Mad Curriculum Disease

E.C. Wragg
Professor of Education
Exeter University

tb
Trentham Books

First published in 1991 by Trentham Books

Trentham Books Limited
13/14 Trent Trading Park
Botteslow Street
Stoke-on-Trent
Staffordshire
England ST1 3LY

British Library Cataloguing in Publication Data
Wragg E. C. (Ted)
  Mad Curriculum Disease
  1. Education. Humour
  I. Title
  370'

ISBN: 0 948080 58 2

Designed and typeset by Trentham Print Design Limited, Chester
and printed in Great Britain by Bemrose Shafron Limited, Chester.

Contents

Chapter 5: Teaching and the image makers

Chapter 6: Priceless primary schools

Chapter 1

Mad Testing Disease

SEAC Recorder: Newsletter No.35

Welcome to Newsletter 35 of the School Examinations and Assessment Council the principle purpose of which, as in the previous 34, is to suggest that we are all one big happy family and that there is nothing nasty about national testing.

Hence the odd bit of Welsh and the many photographs of smiling people holding clipboards and files, clearly having terrific fun.

The only exception is the group captioned 'GCSE examiners marking scripts' showing people sitting round a table covered in test papers. We feature this picture just in case you thought examiners spent their time doing cartwheels.

What is a SAT?

Many teachers have written to SEAC asking if they can see what a Standard Assessment Task (SAT) looks like. There are not many about but one was sighted running across a field near the A1 during that hot spell in July.

As readers will know the purpose of the SATs is to test children's knowledge of the national curriculum through specially devised tests, usually assessing levels in more than one subject. The results of the pilots have not yet been fully analysed but three consortia were each given a third of the National Debt to try out a few ideas. There is currently a keen debate within the Government about the future of national testing. The two options under careful consideration are (a) to give the whole of the gross national product, over a hundred billion pounds, to the newly formed MFOR (Money For Old Rope) consortium to devise tests for the whole population of the United Kingdom on the whole of human knowledge, or (b) just to say 'bugger it' and carry on as usual.

Below is a level 10 SAT piloted with 14-year-olds under the heading 'Snow Across the Curriculum' with the usual subject codes in brackets (eg Ma = maths, Te = technology, Gk = God knows etc).

Snow across the Curriculum
- [ ] Build an igloo (Te)
- [ ] Measure and weigh it (Ma)
- [ ] Write a poem about it (En)
- [ ] Pole vault over it (PE)
- [ ] Melt it (Sc)
- [ ] Say 'Merde, mon igloo est disparu' (ML)

Sop for the Welsh
Pwyllgor Ymgynghorol dros Cgmru (This can be translated as: 'Up yours Dai bach, the Government won't listen to you either').

Changing faces
Mr Silas Wordgrind, formerly copy-writer of Opaque Bulletins Inc, has joined SEAC as Head of Global Communications. His job is to make sure that SEAC newsletters are jargon-free.

He is delighted with his new appointment and has already committed himself to keeping pedagogical operatives aware-briefed on assessment-oriented decision-making situations.

The Secretary of State has announced three new appointments to the important SEAC Committee committee, which receives minutes from the other 78 SEAC committees, including the powerful Who-Created-All-This-Bloody-Stupid-Bureaucracy Committee.

So we welcome *Colonel Adam Smith-Rightwinger,* who fought at Mafeking with the Coldstream Guards, *Ivor Cheek,* principal of Budleigh Salterton City Technology College, and *Bess,* one of the Queen's corgis.

1988 Act made clear
Many teachers have written to SEAC asking about Section 5 (3) of the 1988 Act which states: 'No course of study hereinafter designated as authenticated thereunder shall be provided therewithout by an outside person for pupils of compulsory school age unless approved by the aforementioned Secretary of State'.

In this section:
- [ ] 'Outside person' means a person outside, ie not inside
- [ ] 'an' is the indefinite article when used before a vowel
- [ ] 'age' means how old you are, as in 'I am 10 years of age'

Who does what?

The DES requires SEAC to consult NCC as well as CGLI, NFER, BTEC, BBC, ITV, LBW and C&A about GCSE, CPVE, A and AS and SATS (in Wales TAFFs) based on TGAT.

Subsequently the CBI and TUC comment with the DTI and DOE on training issues which are then conveyed to SEAC and NCC by the GPO. The LEAs report through AMA or ACC to CLEA, except in Yorkshire where they report to EEBYGUM.

Terms explained No.35

Attainment target: This comes from the two words 'attainment' meaning something you reach, like your peak, the sky or the door, and 'target' which is, according to the Oxford English Dictionary, 'a circular stuffed pad' or something you fire or attempt to hit.

Thus 'attainment target' is reaching a state of feeling stuffed, believing you are shooting at the sky, or attempting to hit your head against a door.

Next month: 'Utterly knackered'.

Times Educational Supplement 21.9.90

3

The fractious distillation of SATs and sex

It's been a funny old year, as Jimmy Greaves, Margaret Thatcher, John MacGregor and countless others have no doubt observed. I knew shortly into it that it was not going to be my year, my decade or indeed my century or millennium, come to think of it.

I suppose it must have been the letter I received early in January from some international outfit that started me wondering. It asked what I was doing about 'getting into Europe'. I had thought I was already in it, actually, but I suddenly had the ludicrous vision of catching the boat to Calais, standing on the quayside there and shouting out, 'Right Europe, here I am, so where's the action?'

The idea of 'getting into Europe' always reminds me of that Goon Show episode when Spike Milligan sailed up the Thames and said, 'Hands up England'.

During the year I did attend a couple of brief Euro-binges, though I usually try to avoid them, as they bring out the jingoist in me. Every time the German delegate at one of these Euro-splurges sounds off about how 'we in ze Federal Republic' have got it all sewn up, as if it is some kind of pedagogical Olympics, I always feel like calling out, 'Come off it, Fritz, pull the other one'. Reprehensible, I know, but when one is aware of the reality it is hard to listen to the fantasy.

Back to the present decade, however, for it is now time for the annual awards ceremony. Without doubt or for that matter without serious competition, the daftest document of the year was the School Examinations and Assessment Council's *Guide to Teacher Assessment* packs A,B and C. Three sets of platitudes for the price of one must be good value at any time.

The banality of this triple dose of sleep-inducers hit primary schools like giant concrete blocks back in February. Crash! 'Children do not progress at the same rate.' Thud! 'Teachers do not need reminding that planning is essential. But they may need reminding that it requires time.'

The same documents also contained the most useless piece of advice of the year, namely the tip about how to assess children who were absent from school. Test them more frequently, was the handy tip here, as teachers combed the land, frantically trying to find the little perishers so they could give them even more tests than they were administering to the millions of pupils sitting obediently at their desks.

The best news of the year was the announcement of the ending of the city technology college programme in its original form. The intention that industry would come up with all the money for new buildings never materialised and the Government was forced into the embarrassing position of injecting six, seven or eight million pounds into each CTC building budget, more than it was offering the whole local authority with its hundreds of schools. It was a morally untenable position which John MacGregor had the sense and the decency to recognise.

The Teaching as a Career unit at the DES has made sterling efforts to recruit more teachers, but by contrast the £2.2 million Government- sponsored advertising campaign conducted by Saatchi and Saatchi was the disappointment of the year. After all the preliminary hype we were entitled to expect something distinctly better than the 'It's quite a challenge making fractional distillation more interesting than sex' slogan.

A few years ago some researcher, whose name I forget now, claimed that teachers had a lower sex drive than most other people, and that was before the national curriculum and local management were introduced. The most common reaction from the public to the ad was, 'It's quite a challenge making *what* more interesting than sex?' The reaction from teachers, however, was more likely to be, 'It's quite a challenge making fractional distillation more interesting than *what*?'

The greatest mystery of the year was why the national press and broadcasting media suddenly went mad about educational standards in the summer. It cannot be explained by the silly-season theory alone, because it has persisted well beyond that flat 'phew, what a scorcher!' period in July and August.

Most noteworthy has been the ranting style of many newspaper leaders. Even papers normally fair in their education news coverage, seem to have a leader-writer who is wheeled out of a cupboard from time to time to pen a retired Colonel-style splutter. One journalist explained it to me by saying that these leader-writers were all public school boys who were frantically trying to justify their own private education by slagging off the state system, but I cannot believe it is that simple.

Getting good news into the national press is a problem. The SEAC report on national testing in maths by the Assessment of Performance Unit between 1984 and 1988, was reported as more evidence of falling standards, because the scores of 11 year-olds had gone down in the number tests. In all the four other areas, geometry, measures, probability/statistics and algebra, scores had actually gone *up,* something few reported.

Good guy of the year must be John MacGregor, who endured considerable abuse from his party for listening to what practitioners were saying. For this he was accused of having 'gone native'. It is astonishing that the act of consulting the people who do a job should be condemned as wimpish collusion, rather than acclaimed as sensible management.

But what about 1991 and the future? Perhaps the most notable feature of this coming year will be the piloting of the national testing programme. At last we shall find out what a standard assessment task really is. The funniest moment I can recall in 1990 was at the annual conference of the United Kingdom Reading Association, when Colin Harrison announced to the audience that he had brought with him a real live SAT.

Faced with this rare opportunity to learn something about the unknown, people leaned forward expectantly in their seats. Colin thereupon put a large black bin-liner over his head, donned rubber gloves and then drew gently out of a holdall a small parcel using an enormous pair of tongs. It made the point beautifully about the eternal mystery of SAT's and the sense of contamination that will accompany them as a result. Never in the history of educational testing can so many have known so little about so much. Happy New Year.

Times Educational Supplement 28.12.90

Little Twinky sorts the sheep from the goats

Head: Ah, come in Mrs Jenkins and sit down. Now, it's about your Melvin's test scores, isn't it? What can I tell you about them?

Mrs J: Well, headmaster, I'm confused about our Melvin's national test scores, so I thought I'd ask if you could explain it all to me, like you said you would at parents' evening if there was anything we didn't understand.

H: Of course, of course, Mrs Jenkins. As I said, this is the first time round for all of us, and we'll just have to feel our way, So what was it you wanted to talk about, his maths scores was it?

Mrs J: It was all of them, really. I don't understand the whole thing. Why are you giving him all these tests, he's only seven?

H: It's not us, you understand, Mrs Jenkins. These are national tests for seven-year-olds, and we have to give them by law. It was all in the 1988 Education Act.

Mrs J: Well, what about these government set books? I know some parents have bought them all. Mrs Fforbes Ffrench just sent the chauffeur to the bookshop and bought the lot, but we couldn't afford £250, so we got him *Little Twinky Goes To Toyland* for Christmas and his grandma bought him *Little Twinky Goes to a City Technology College* for his birthday.

H: I must stress that these are not set books, and ministers have said that parents should not go out and buy them. The Government simply published a set of titles, 27 books for level two and 24 for level three, on which the tests will be based. The ones you mention are both level two, and books like *Little Twinky Makes a Fortune in the Futures Market* are level three.

Mrs J: But I still don't understand all this levels business, headmaster. Melvin's gran keeps asking me if he's passed his exams, and I don't know what to tell her. Algernon Fforbes Ffrench got a three for his set books on the tests, and I know for a fact he's been getting private coaching, but our Melvin only got a two. Does that mean he's failed?

H: I must repeat Mrs Jenkins these are not set books and I am sorry Mrs Fforbes Ffrench has hired a private tutor, but you see a level two means that Melvin is average for his age and Algernon is above average.

Mrs J: Well, why didn't Melvin get a three? We tried to help him with his course work, but I think Algernon's tutor does more than we do.

H: I think I can explain that to you. Let's have a look at Melvin's written work. I have here his essay for what the Government calls 'standard assessment tasks' for seven-year-olds. The title was, 'Compare and contrast the books in the Little Twinky series as allegories of successful capitalism'. Your Melvin wrote, 'I like Little Twinky, He is very nice. The Allegro is my grandad's car, and the capital is London'. Whereas Algernon's essay began, 'The Little Twinky series stands firmly in the traditions of symbolic representation of meaning through narrative, exemplified by, among others, John Bunyan'.

Mrs J: So our Melvin did fail then?

H: No Mrs Jenkins, he got a level two which is average for seven-year-olds.

Mrs J: But he got a two in all his English grades and in maths and in all his science. It says here in his report that he got two for genetics, two for electricity and magnetism, two for earth sciences and two for astronomy.

H: Yes, we felt he had really performed well. There was a tremendous sense of two-ness about everything he did. You must look on the positive side of this. His two in genetics, for example, was an excellent two, right at the top end of the twos. You can be proud of Melvin. He was outstandingly average across the board. Think of it more as an Upper Second.

Mrs J: But he's had no lessons at all in school for the last month because of all these tests. And where is his history grade? You see when we read in the papers about the history national curriculum and topics like 'Study the building technology of the pyramids and the Parthenon', his dad knocked grandad's garage down so he and Melvin could build a pyramid-shaped one with pillars in the front, but now grandad can't get his Allegro into it.

H: Ah, I can explain that. The national curriculum has been simplified and there are no longer any tests in history.

Mrs J: There's another thing we're worried about. It's this story in the *Swinesville Globe*. They've printed the league table with all the scores. I've got it here. Look, the headline says, 'Swinesville bottom of league'. Then it goes on, 'The parents of Swinesville county primary school must be sick as a parrot to find their children are the dunces of Swineshire in the league table of national test scores assembled by *Swinesville Globe* reporters. Chairman of governors, garage-owner Ned Nock aged 55, said that he would be seeing the headmaster today to sort things out. The *Globe* says 'Make the lazy pupils of Swinesville primary pull their socks up, Mr Nock, and while you're on with it, tell the teachers to get on their bikes'.

H: You must understand that such league tables are unofficial. If we had only had more pupils like your Melvin, Mrs Jenkins, we would have been higher up the league. You will be pleased to hear that we have got a new policy for the future at Swinesville primary. We want to aim for nothing less than to get off the bottom of the league table and be safely in the middle where we belong.

Mrs J: Is there anything we can do to help?

H: Yes indeed. We see your Melvin as a model for the future. Under the slogan, 'You too for a two', we intend every single child to get a solid row of twos, so we shall be looking carefully at our selection procedures. There are two things you can do to help. As we can't at present afford all the Little Twinky series, I'd like you to help run a bazaar and raffle which might even raise enough money to buy multiple copies of all the set books. The second thing is that if you and Mr Jenkins could possibly breed a few more Melvins, I'd be over the moon, Mrs Jenkins, over the moon.

Times Educational Supplement 25.1.91

The Relapse ...or Carry On Testing

I was cured. Straight up, I was pronounced completely clear of all Mad Curriculum Disease symptoms, not a twitch, clean bill of health. Then look what happened. I went along to my first SAT training conference and here I am, back in a packed Mad Curriculum Disease isolation ward, alongside all the other participants, lurching round hysterically in my carpet slippers, sniggering uncontrollably.

We inmates now spend most of our day muttering meaningless jargon and filling anything square-shaped with endless ticks and digits. I got put in solitary yesterday for entering a row of twos in Biro on the consultant's check shirt. Apparently I was just jibbering, 'But you're average, man', before they sedated me and put me away for the night.

I knew it had started as soon as I received my briefing pack from the School Examinations and Assessment Council. I would have written to Philip Halsey, the chairman and chief executive of SEAC, thanking him, but it came in a parcel about two inches thick containing somewhere between 200 and 300 photocopied pages of unadulterated bureaucratic twaddle. Honestly, Phil, my finely tuned electronic tripe-detector just emitted a single high-pitched whine before congealing into a shapeless blob of molten metal and plastic.

Perhaps it was because my pack fell open at a wad labelled *School Assessment Folder Part Seven,* which begins with a belter, a comprehension-defying section telling me about the Education (National Curriculum) (Assessment Arrangements for English, Mathematics and Science) Order 1990 and the Education (National Curriculum (Assessment Arrangements in English, Welsh, Mathematics and Science) (Wales) Order 1990. I wish you had sent me the Welsh version, Phil, it might have been clearer.

This gem is in a section headed *What you Must Do,* which orders me to complete documents A and C. It is written in a cheery tone and says things like, 'You might also find that documents B and D are helpful in completing A and C.' The more the merrier I always say.

What shocked me is that, by the time it got into its stride, this particular text had scaled heights never before attained, even during manned space flight: 'When the results for each girl have been transferred, count up how many girls attained each level, and enter the totals at the right hand side of the form. For each attainment target, profile component and subject, check that the totals for D,N,W,1,2 and 3 add up to the total number of girls in Year 2. For Ma 6 the totals for D,N,L,2 and 3 should add up to the total number of girls in Year 2. Repeat the process for boys.' That's top drawer, Phil, world class.

Trying to remind myself that this was all about seven-year-old children, not someone's plan to forecast eight score draws on next Saturday's football pools, I turned next to the Teacher's Book. May I suggest a government health warning here Phil, saying something like, 'Warning: Opening this book can cause a fatal bout of uncontrolled mirth'?

Take for example Ma 1, to use the bizarre language of these things, which is the first maths task. My instructions say, 'Place all forty counters in two unequal piles. Ask the children which of the two piles of counters would make the longer straight line if the counters were arranged end to end'. No sweat, Phil. Thirty-nine in one pile, one in the other. That should bump up the school's batting average in the league table.

Off now to Sc 5, or science as you and I used to call it when life was simpler. This one is about 'Things we throw away', and I am instructed, 'Ask the children to tell you about the kinds of things that they would expect to find in a dustbin/waste bin/refuse sack'. No problem round here. The bins are so full of SEAC documents there's no room for much else.

English is equally rich. En 1 (you can be proud of me, even with Mad Curriculum Disease I still remember the code book) instructs me to 'Plan some games that require children to give each other instructions'. One crisp suggestion is to blindfold children and then get them to give each other instructions about how to reach an object. Thanks, Phil, you're a pal. I can just see it: 'Left a bit, right a bit, no not there you fool, come back, A-a-a-r-g-h'.

Has anyone at SEAC the slightest understanding of the reality of trying out all these capers with a classroom full of seven-year-old livewires? I can just see the people wandering round with their clipboard giving meaningless marks based on eavesdropping on casual conversations during an unspecified game. I tried out poker. Apart from losing about 20 quid it was not too bad, Phil, but how do you score, 'Hit me for three', 'See your 10 and raise you 10', or 'I'm all cleaned out, pass me another Heineken'?

Incidentally, I had a pantomine with Level 2, Part D on En 1; you remember, the bit about assessing 'talk with the teacher'. I was not sure how many qualified for Level 2 in the section where I have to 'Observe children who show, by their facial expression or posture, that they are listening to what you say'. Darren sat throughout my talk with his tongue out, Melanie stood on her head, and Gary held up a sheet of paper on which he had written 'Artistic impression — minus 1.5'. Algernon Fforbes-Ffrench is cross-eyed, so I was not sure whether he was looking at me or the radiator.

Finally the documentation. The sad thing is, Phil, that a few of these tasks would actually be quite interesting to do. Weed out the dafter ones, cut back on the paperwork, and it might be a runner. But the page upon page of squared and lined paper, the sheet after sheet, row upon row, column after column, are simply too much for seven-year-olds, too much for their teachers and the degree of detail is way over the top.

All this is screamingly obvious now, let alone after this year's pilots. The whole programme in its present form is crackers, mad, loony, screwy, potty, completely nuts. It reads more like a script for the latest British comedy *Carry On Testing*. Do we really have to put schools through the wringer in the summer term with the inevitable turmoil that will produce?

The saddest thing of all is that when heads and others have been to their training sessions, they and thousands of teachers who are perfectly competent at their job will feel that they must be failures because (a) the whole exercise is so complex and detailed, and (b) the documentation is crippling.

It will be the fault of the system not of themselves, but the Mad Curriculum Disease isolation wards will still be full to overflowing.

Times Educational Supplement 22.2.91

News *from the Department of Education and Science:*

Academic/vocational divide ended

The Government has decided to end the division between academic and vocational courses at 16-plus. The decision was announced in a White Paper entitled *Same as Usual: a New Beginning.* The Government's proposals will simplify what has often been called the 'post-16 jungle'. In the most radical reform of sixth form education this century, pupils will in future be able to take a brand new Advanced Diploma.

Announcing this radical change, Mr Kenneth Clarke said, 'If that man in the glasses and grey suit would mind sitting down so that I can have my turn, as we arranged beforehand, I would like to say that this is the most exciting development in education since I last spoke. In future, all sixth formers who wish to do so, and are clever, will be able to undertake really high level work in several academic subjects of their choice, well, three actually, and obtain the new *Advanced Diploma in A levels* as we shall be calling it. Those who do not mind getting their hands dirty will go to places which are, I believe, known as colleges of furtive education, and take the *Advanced Diploma in Vocational (definitely not A level) Education* in subjects like, I suppose, plumbing, or bus driving, or whatever these places do.

'This plan, which I thought up entirely by myself last night, will not only take us into the 20th century but also enable us to compete with our competitors like Liechtenstein and Albania. It is a far-reaching reform, and its most radical feature is that it leaves everything exactly the same as it was before. To those cynics who ask me what I understand by 'vocational education' I can only reply, 'Search me'.'

Curriculum simplified

The Government has announced that the national curriculum is to be simplified. The number of attainment targets will be reduced in subjects such as maths and science. Mr Kenneth Clarke said, 'There are far too many attainment targets around nowadays I intend to cut the number, as soon as I find out what they actually are. I am told that there are 17 in science and 14 in maths and I cannot imagine which fool introduced so many. Kenneth who? Well, nevertheless I'm going to cut them down to eight. Yes eight, ladies and

13

gentlemen. No, I tell you what, make it seven. Look, I like your face missus, to you six. All right, call me barmy, I'm giving these away today, five, that's my final offer, five attainment targets. Now, who'd like some? Couple of nice SATs for the wife sir, while you're on with it? They're lovely and fresh, only used once.'

Recent HMSO publications
- [ ] *Cutting Down the Amount of Paper We Send to Schools* — Vol 1 (260pp) £19.95
- [ ] *Cutting Down the Amount of Paper We Sentdto Schools* — Vol 2 (260pp) £19.95
- [ ] *White Paper 1 Same as Usual: A New Beginning* (2pp + very shiny cover) £5
- [ ] *White Paper 2 Take the Money and Run Squire: the Training Credit Scheme Explained* (2pp + glossy cover) £1,000 (used tenners, straight into your bank account, no questions asked)
- [ ] *Fancy a Brand New Building? —A Guide to Opting Out* (20pp) name your price.

Curriculum update
The national curriculum is to be simplified, Mr Kenneth Clarke has announced. Speaking at a press conference, he said, 'Who the hell decided to have five attainment targets in science anyway? Oh, it was me was it? Well I'm cutting them down to four, no, I tell a lie, three. Let's call them biology, physics and chemistry. In fact, after a widespread consultative process, I have been advised by the chap who sits in the corner of the saloon bar at the Dog and Partridge — you know the one, the red-faced bloke, always sticks to draught Guinness — that we only need one. Yes sirree, one's plenty. Call it 'science'. Brilliant'.

The following statutory orders replace previous science statutory orders:
- [ ] Level 1 Do some science
- [ ] Level 2 Do more science
- [ ] Level 3 Do even more science
- [ ] Level 4 Spell 'science'.
- [ ] Level 5 Do quite a bit of science, if you think about it
- [ ] Level 6 Do the sort of science your dad won't understand
- [ ] Level 7 Do the sort of science we used to do at school, you know, with test tubes and things
- [ ] Level 8 Do a terrific amount of science

☐ Level 9 Do experiments where you have to draw diagrams using those plastic rectangles with cut-out shapes like Bunsen burners
☐ Level 10 Do science which involves coloured liquids in those funny things with a round glass bowl and a long spout ('retorts', is it?)

National tests simplified

The Government has announced that national tests for seven-year-olds, will be simplified. A SEAC spokesman said, 'The evaluation of this year's SATs (*The Kids Loved It, Honest* (2pp + lurex covers) — HMSO £19.95) has shown that of the 600,000 pupils who sat the SATs, satting was successfully achieved with a majority of the satted sattees. Next year semi-satting will result in a sattable majority being sub-satted by experienced satters'. Mr Kenneth Clarke said, 'I am proposing to reduce the tests to just maths (a long division sum will do here) and a spelling test, probably a single word like 'accommodate' or 'committee', which are quite good teasers I've always found.'

Stop press

The national curriculum is to be simplified, the Government has announced. Mr Kenneth Clarke said, 'I tell you what, why don't we just have one attainment target. I know, we could call it 'Education'. Brilliant. Just a minute, I've got a better idea...

Times Educational Supplement 31.5.91

The brat sat on the mat

Tim and his tests: a new graded reading scheme for primary schools

Book 1:
Tim had a test. It was called a SAT. He got it from Ken. Tim and Ken are men. Tim likes his test. 'My test is best,' says Tim. 'Tim has a good test,' says Ken, 'I like his test. It is the best.' Ken likes a pub. He likes his grub. He likes grub in a pub. But he likes Tim's test the best. 'Rub a dub dub. I like grub in a pub,' says Ken, 'but Tim's test is the best.'

Book 2:
Pat is a head. Matt is a head. Nat is a head. They are all heads. Pat is mad. She is very mad. She is very, very mad. 'Tim's test is bad,' says Pat. 'I am sad,' says Matt. 'Tim is a bad cad,' says Nat. 'Tim is a bad, bad, lad,' says Pat. 'His test is a fad'. 'I will tell his dad,' says Matt, 'Tim and Ken are mad, bad lads.' 'By gad, I am sad,' says Nat. Pat, Matt and Nat are all sad heads.

Book 3:
Tim's test is a SAT. It takes a long time. Pat is in her prime. 'Tim's test is slime,' says Pat, 'It is not worth a dime.' 'My test is fine,' says Tim. 'Do not pine. I must draw the line.' 'Then draw the line fine,' says Matt, 'under your SAT.' 'Put your SAT under your mat,' says Nat, 'Or give it to the cat.' 'Please do not whine,' says Tim. 'My SAT is fine. What's more, it's all mine.' 'The heads do not shine,' says Ken. 'I like wine from the vine when I dine in the pub.'

Book 4:
Pat, Matt and Nat were once like a lat. But now they get fat. They used to drink shorts, but now they drink vats. 'Tim's SAT is tat,' said Pat, 'and he is a brat.' 'Ken is a prat,' said Matt.

    'What did you do with your SAT?' asked Nat. 'I hit my SAT with a bat,' said Pat. 'I sat on my SAT,' said Matt. 'I shat on my SAT,' said Nat. Nat was rude. He was a rude dude. He wanted to be rude to Ken and Tim, so he was hoping to be elected president of the National Association of Headteachers one day.

Book 5:

'Bong, bong,' said Pat, hitting Tim with a gong. 'Your test is too long. It has a pong and it is wrong.' 'My test is not too long,' said Tim. 'It is just right.' 'It is not bright,' said Matt, 'it gave me a fright. Don't be so tight.' 'Talk to a kid,' said Nat, 'Then you'll get rid.'

Tim talked to three kids. 'I'm level 1. I'm thick,' said Dick. 'I'm level 2. I'm slick,' said Nick. 'I'm level 3. I'm sick,' said Marmaduke Ffrench-Fitz-warren, 'but that's because my parents assiduously bought all the set books, made me learn them off by heart and what is more, paid several thousand pounds for a private tutor — and I was rather hoping to be level 4, but what do you expect in this regrettably egalitarian age?'

Book 6:

'I've got an idea,' said Tim to Ken. 'I wish I had an idea,' said Ken to Tim. 'Can I have your idea?' 'No you can't,' said Tim crossly, 'It's my idea. I thought of it first.' 'All right,' said Ken. 'Tell me your idea and then we'll have some grub in the pub.'

'Well, you know how the SAT took up half a term,' said Tim. 'Did it?' said Ken, 'By the way, what's a SAT?' 'Don't worry,' said Tim, 'you're better off not knowing. Anyway, I'm going to say that it was the teachers' own fault, because they wanted this kind of test.'

'I thought it was your test,' said Ken. 'No, it was really supposed to be your test,' said Tim, 'but we won't go into all that now. Look, I'm going to tell the teachers it will be easier next year. I'll make it last a whole term instead.'

'But isn't a whole term longer than a half term?' asked Ken. 'Yes, of course it is,' replied Tim. 'So won't that make it... ,' he paused for about half an hour counting first on his fingers and then on his toes, '...about three times as long?' 'Twice as long actually,' said Tim. 'So won't teachers have to be pretty silly to believe that it's going to be any better next year then?' asked Ken. 'Very silly indeed,' said Tim.

'Let's go to the pub for some grub,' said Ken. 'Let's eat the same amount of grub, but take twice as long over it. That way we'll get slim,' said Tim. 'You're a clever begger, Eggar,' said Ken.

A real book:

'Where a pupil is unable to complete a SAT due to his absence from school... if in the opinion of his headteacher he has not done enough work as aforesaid, the levels of attainment determined by the teacher assessment shall be the levels for the purpose of article 7 unless the local education authority (in the case of a pupil at a school which the authority maintain) or SEAC (in the case of a pupil at a grant-maintained school) disagree, in which case the levels of attainment shall be such as the local authority or SEAC determine by reference to the work the pupil has done on the SAT in question.'

From *The Education (National Curriculum) (Assessment Arrangements in English, Mathematics and Science) (Key Stage 1)* Order, a document sent to all LEAs and other organisations by the Department of Education and Science to clarify the forms of assessment of seven-year-olds in the three core subjects, and also in technology, in 1992.

Times Educational Supplement 14.6.91

Chapter 2

Ken and Ken

Genghis Ken, life and soul of the saloon bar

I have been reading up the new topic which has just been added to the national curriculum history syllabus. It is in the legally 'essential' or 'Hello Strangeways if you don't do it' category. I refer, of course, to the 11 years of the Educan Dynasty during the Great Imperial Miss Piggi Era.

This age began peacefully with the ascendancy of Mark the Silent, who was soon overthrown and replaced by Joseph the Mad, also known as Joseph the Engaging Loon. Following the downfall of Joseph the Mad, a new ruler, Kenneth the Spiv, assumed the throne. He believed that society could only be saved by a return to the ways of the ancients, so he introduced ancestor worship and the adoration of the Supreme Being Miss Piggi.

During the reign of Kenneth the Spiv there were many wars as he sought to place increasing emphasis on ceremonies and rituals revering the past. He introduced a feudal system and elaborate records, requiring calligraphers to spend thousands of hours compiling millions of sheets of writing.

After this period of disunion and domestic dissension the next Emperor, Mac the Peacemaker, sought to heal the many divisions by welding his subjects into a single cult, but his reign was short-lived and he was succeeded by a ruler from another land, Kenneth the Teenage Mutant Ninja Turtle. His relationship with his former subjects has been greatly influenced by the precepts of Genghis Khan. Since there was a strong rumour, for a time, that Mac the Peacemaker was to be succeeded by Norman Tebbit, also known as Norm-An the Cruel, I would have settled for Vlad the Impaler.

What put me off about Kenneth the Ninja, apart from his insulting of doctors, shabby treatment of nurses, contempt for ambulance workers, closure of hospital wards, slavish adherence to market ideology, and those are just a few of his good points, was the assertion that he was the sort of bloke you would expect to meet in a pub. You can meet some very rum coves in pubs.

I am already pig sick of all the medics I know coming up to me, collapsing with hysterical glee and then skipping happily down the road to the nearest pub, hoping no doubt to find him there, so that they can congratulate him on his move and say how much they will miss him. I hope he is less of an apparatchik than he seems to be.

One certainty is that the Ninja will find there is no shortage of advice about what he should do to improve things. First, he will be told that he must under no circumstances, 'go native'. This is what is said to have happened to John MacGregor by critics in his own party. Yet all he did was join that somewhat sizeable group of humanity, consisting of all those in possession of more than 10 brain cells, which realised that testing seven-year-olds on the nine academic subjects and 60 or 70 attainment targets was not completely sensible.

Next, he will be urged to describe opting out as the jewel in the crown. If opting out is the jewel then it must be a pretty shabby crown.

The first opted-out secondary schools have been given 10-15 times as much money for school buildings as maintained schools, in what is probably the major scandal of the past few years. They are also being offered what will no doubt be one-off cash inducements. A few of the more gullible appear to believe that they too will be in receipt of huge bounties if they opt out.

Anyone with an atom of sense must realise that, were all schools to opt out, the Government would not dream of multiplying tenfold what it gives to schools. These extra payments are what is known in lay terms as bribes or backhanders, and anyone who believes the bonanza will go on forever should just compare the funding that schools get through the Technical and Vocational Education Initiative with the huge grants to the first few schools seven years ago. The most likely outcome of spreading opting out to all primary schools is great embarrassment.

Small schools of 50 pupils or less will try to opt out when threatened with closure by local authorities implementing the Government's rationalisation policies.

The many fringe pressure groups will want their say. I see that the Adam Smith Institute has suggested the establishment of a *Good School Guide,* on the lines of the *Good Food Guide.* I can't wait for all that pretentious stuff about lessons suffused with just a soupcon of aromatic whatever, and school canteens gaining the much-coveted maximum of five Rennies for cuisine and three spittoons for ambience.

The jewel in the crown, so to speak, of advice comes, I believe, from Oliver Letwin. I am told that Young Olly, former adviser to Keith Joseph and Miss Piggy, believes that the answer to our problems is to revive the school song. I would have expected no less from the great man. Let us get down to essentials. When your back is against the wall, your shoulder firmly applied to the wheel, your upper lip suitably stiffened and your teeth firmly gritted, have a good sing I always say, even at the risk of a double hernia.

So for Young Olly and all the traditionalists, and to welcome the Ninja aboard, I humbly offer my own freshly-composed school song to cure all our ills.

Floreat Little Piddington Church
of England Combined Junior and
Infant School,
There's no room
For much else
In this song,
So don't opt out,
Just floreat Little Piddington Church
of England Combined Junior and
Infant School.

It has a morale boosting ring to it. There is also the added advantage for traditionalists that an early start can be made on grammar, as teachers explain to the new five-year-olds that *floreat* is the present subjunctive of a second conjugation Latin verb.

Times Educational Supplement 16.11.90

21

Scouts asked to do silly jobs for their DES bobs

Do you ever get that feeling that you can't keep up, that things are sprinting ahead of you? We used to have a magnificent Alsatian who was quite fast on his feet. One day in the local park he decided to chase a greyhound. Unable to get within 50 yards of it, for the first and only time in his life he gave up the chase and sat down, watching in admiration as his athletic playmate raced effortlessly and at enormous speed round and round the perimeter.

It was the canine equivalent of taking his hat off to it, and that was precisely how I felt a couple of weeks ago when I read with growing horror and then mirth, of the Government's plans to introduce a national curriculum for the Scouts, Guides, Boys' Brigade and other youth organisations. Honestly, even at my daftest I would not have suggested satirising the national curriculum by pretending it would be applied to the Peewit patrol in the local Scout troop. When it comes to scaling the utmost heights of lyrical lunacy, we ordinary mortals, like my Alsatian, just have to stop short of the pinnacle and leave the final ascent to the real experts.

It is all true, I'm afraid. Education Ministers have announced that they want more 'value for money' in return for the £2 million a year grant given to youth organisations. In order to qualify for cash in future, according to newspaper accounts of a private meeting held last month, it will be goodbye to making your own woggle and then toasting it on the camp fire, or whatever we used to do, and hello to what are called 'new standards of financial efficiency' and 'meeting objectives approved by the Government'. Lord Baden-Powell must be turning in his vault.

In retrospect I think I learned a lot from the Cubs, the Scouts and the local youth club without any Government interference at all. In terms of the inevitable 'value for money' criterion, all the youth groups have made incalculable contributions to society from keeping people off the streets and out of mischief to inculcating the tenets of good citizenry. I don't think I can ever forget the statement I and countless others made over and over again, to be a friend to all and a brother to every other Scout, no matter to what country, class or creed the other may belong. It was not a bad aspiration.

The Minister who made the announcement about more Government control said: 'This is not intended to be a strait-jacket into which organisations and activities should fit. It should be a broad framework.' The statement echoed almost to the letter a speech about the national curriculum by Kenneth Baker two years earlier. There are no details of what this latest wizard wheeze will look like in practice, but one possible draft from a Government-backed source suggests it should include such matters as writing a curriculum vitae, applying for a job and understanding housing benefit rules, as well as political education and what is called 'sexual self-awareness'.

Now hold it right there sunshine. Before all that is sacred floats gently down the Swanee, leading me and thousands of others to return our hard-won Leaping Wolf badges in disgust, let us just have a teeny peek at this particular set of attainment targets. I can just imagine the reaction of my mates all those years ago if, instead of learning to be self-sufficient in the only wood round our parts that hadn't been choked by industrial smog, and then happily singing 'Ging Gang Goolie' around the camp fire, we had been forced to fill in imaginary job application forms and listen to someone from the Town Hall drone on about housing benefits.

As for 'sexual self-awareness', well, I can only say that I prefer the innocence of yesteryear to some Government-approved lecturette on what the dangly bits are for. If there was one thing we were explicitly *not* made aware of in my day it was sex. As we quietly sipped our bromide-laced cocoa our minds were on higher things, like how to get our Bushman's Thong. I wonder if, in future, instead of tramping up to London to collect their Queen's Scout badge, the Peewit patrol will have to go to the DES instead and say to ministers: 'We now know what the plumbing is for, so can we have the loot?'

Where will it all end? Will youth groups be run by governing bodies dominated by businessmen checking out whether they have met their performance targets and marking their job application forms out of 10? Will there be new badges to strive for, like the Stockbroker Badge? And will there be 10 levels for each attainment target and working parties on cross-curricular themes? If so, how can you combine sexual self-awareness and filling in a curriculum vitae? The mind boggles.

I think I have the hang of new-style scouting, so I have designed a Government-approved First Class badge. The requirements are as follows:

- ☐ Rub two cabinet ministers together to make a fire.
- ☐ Help out for a week at the office of a local estate agent.
- ☐ Do a good deed every day, like expose a welfare state scrounger.
- ☐ During Bob-a-Job week, demand a sweetener on top of the bob. Spend the money on electricity shares.

☐ Write an essay on, 'Mrs Thatcher, genius or saviour of the nation?'
☐ Camp in a French farmer's field. Say *in English*. 'Hellow garlic breath, when are you frogs going to become efficient?' Then tell him where to put his butter mountain.

It is, of course, tempting for Governments to want to control the minds and woggles of the nation's youth, but can't they stay out of the dob, dob, dob, business, and leave it to its innocence?

Times Educational Supplement 5.10.90

"HOLD IT! YOU'VE PUT THAT ONE'S EYE BROWS ON UPSIDE. DOWN ..."

Of mad dogs and education ministers...

Have you heard the story about the World's most intelligent dog competition — staged to find the most intelligent dog in the world? Three finalists appeared with their proud owners and paraded up and down before the most senior judge in the world, seated at a table bearing a magnificent gleaming silver championship trophy.

The distinguished judge stood up and announced to the huge audience the details of the final and decisive test the dogs would have to complete. The three dogs and their owners, an engineer, a sculptor and a government minister, listened attentively as the judge explained that a hundred bones would be laid on the floor. Whichever dog assembled these into the most interesting and complex construction would win the priceless silver trophy and the title of Most Intelligent Dog in the World.

The first competitor, the engineer, stepped forward. 'Brunel, Brunel, go boy,' he called, and the dog immediately raced into the arena, scuttled hither and thither among the bones, and assembled the most intricate model of a suspension bridge. The crowd thundered applause and the judge, seated at his table, made copious approving notes.

Next the sculptor strode into the ring. 'Epstein, Epstein, go boy,' he yelled, and the second eager dog raced over to the pile of bones and fashioned an incredibly lifelike head and shoulders bust of Beethoven. There were gasps from the crowd. Surely the silver trophy had already been won.

Finally the government minister came forward. 'Bullshit, Bullshit, go boy,' he called, whereupon the third dog strolled into the arena, ate all the bones, bit the judge, widdled on the table leg, picked up the trophy and went home for the rest of the day.

I tell this story not merely as a round about way of saying all government ministers are superficial, opportunist, contemptuous and indolent, because although some are, others are industrious, concerned and self-effacing, but rather because I am perplexed about the behaviour of some education ministers of late.

Our ministers tend to get a relatively short time in office, though it is not as bad as in some countries. Although being Secretary of State is a high-profile job, being a junior minister can have as much impact as a speck of snow landing on Alaska. Remember Joe Thing and Harry Whatsit, or was it Joe Whatsit and Harry Thing? No? Neither do I. The more forgettable did their greatest service to education when they resigned.

I have been racking my brains to work out what is afoot with our current crop of ministers. During the extensive debates on the 1944 Education Act, R A Butler was at pains to point out that he had no intention of interfering in the school curriculum. This promise was repeated, though with much less conviction, by Kenneth Baker when the 1988 Act was going through Parliament. He pointed out that schools would be cushioned from political interference by various councils for curriculum and examinations.

So why then is Mr Clarke laying down the law about the content of geography, history or any other subject? Why does a politician decide, for example, the place of skills in a subject like geography, saying that there is less need for these since they are taught in other subjects? Fair enough, I suppose. I often do mapping in my music lessons.

I can now reveal the true purpose of much recent ministerial behaviour, and it is this. I know you will find this hard to believe, but the reason is that *ministers intend to teach the national curriculum themselves.*

Shocked? I thought you might be, but look at the evidence. A couple of weeks ago junior minister Michael Fallon, a member of the No Turning Up Group, produced a league table of all local authorities, ranked according to their exam results at 16 plus.

This was said by many to be a cheap political trick, because, as everyone knows, social class correlates highly with exam success, so those authorities with more socially privileged children, often in Conservative areas, will usually outscore those in depressed areas, which are often Labour-controlled. Only fools take these unadjusted league tables seriously and Professor John Gray of Sheffield University has shown that if you partial out the social class element the picture changes dramatically.

However, I can reveal that good old Mike's real purpose in this exercise was to teach maths national curriculum attainment target nine (using and applying mathematics), level seven, which states, 'follow a chain of mathematical reasoning, spotting inconsistencies... make a collection of graphs or charts from daily newspapers; consider whether any of them are misleading'. Thanks Mike, nice lesson plan.

Then there was Mr Clarke at the North of England Conference, playing his Genghis Ken role as the thinking man's thug. He managed to get a round of booing when asked about the bribes he was offering to schools to opt out by suggesting that, if the audience thought the Government would soon stop the hand-outs once they had most schools in their grasp, they should get their application in quickly. That was design and technology attainment target four (appraising), level four: 'Review the judgements they have made in achieving their final artefacts.'

On this shabby opting-out issue, it was the parents of Devon's King Edward VI School, Totnes, who did the best national curriculum implementation. Despite all ministerial offers, they produced their own booklet entitled, 'No thank you, Mr Clarke', and then sensibly voted by an overwhelming majority against opting out. This fulfilled history attainment target three (acquiring and evaluating historical information), level three,' 'reorganise and comment on the amount of information provided by different sources ... recognise fictional aspects ... gross exaggeration of the achievement ... or distortion'. Nice one, parents.

Times Educational Supplement 8.2.91

One-man act of the terrible duo

There is nothing like a spell as Secretary of State for turning an ordinary harmless chap into a complete megalomaniac. John MacGregor was the only one in recent times not to succumb. The rest remind me in varying degrees of a local loon, who used to frequent the football ground I attended as a child and call out to the players during every attack, 'All in a straight line now, I'm in charge,' before bursting into high-pitched laughter.

Although Sir Keith Joseph started to take more central control, over grants for inservice training of teachers and non advanced further education, it was Kenneth Baker who changed the job from one that had little direct power beyond the ability to close down temporary buildings in school yards, to one that had more than 400 powers to control curriculum, testing and a host of other matters.

Many were afraid of such powers including, among other distinguished predecessors, R A Butler who saw the wisdom of keeping politics out of the classroom. During the second reading of the 1988 Education Reform Bill Edward Heath said: 'The Secretary of State has taken more powers under the Bill than any other member of the Cabinet, more than my right honourable friends the Chancellor of the Exchequer, the Secretary of State for Defence and the Secretary of State for Social Services.'

All this personal power clearly went to the head of Kenneth Baker as it has done to Kenneth Clarke. In fact, did you realise that the two of them are actually one and the same person? If you notice, they are rarely seen together, and even when they are sitting near each other during televised sessions of Parliament, it is devilishly difficult to detect which is the inflatable and which the one-man double act.

Even though Kenneth Baker-Clarke is now at the Home Office, he still thinks he is in charge of education and has to slag off teachers. A couple of weeks ago, talking about crime and criminals he said in a radio interview, 'If you want to know what creates crime then you have to go back to the heart of our schooling, what happens in Britain's schools.'

I can't wait for the Old Greasepot to start his power-crazed rampage through the prison system, with a national curriculum for burglars, and privatised jails where warders carry glow-in-the-dark personalised Snoopy truncheons that play 'My Way' when you bonk someone on the head with them. I am glad he has ended slopping out for teachers though. Long overdue.

Kenneth Clarke-Baker, on the other hand, has taken advantage of his immense powers to become an expert on the place of factual information in history one week, on the acquisition of skills in geography the next, and an unlikely expert on physical education, when he vetoes the proposal that all 11 year olds should learn to swim 25 metres. I await eagerly his wise pronouncements on Bach, Beethoven. and the role of batik in art. Such a polymath is wasted at the Department of Education and Science. He should be winning *Brain of Britain, Mastermind* and the Booker Award in his spare time, between knocking off a few Nobel prizes, Olympic gold medals, and being Poet Laureate.

His latest wheeze is to propose that all schools should be automatically opted out and have to vote to opt into local authorities. Compulsion is always the final means of bolstering a flagging or clapped-out idea. Yet no proper thought has been given to the possible consequences of having the complete opt out that he and others seek.

If the Government has no faith in local authorities, then why does it not do the honest thing and just kill them off? I can see some weaknesses in local education authorities, but I should hate to have what would effectively be a nationalised education service, with each school nothing more than a file in the DES. Anyone who has been in the DES, or dealt with Whitehall departments, can testify to the nightmare there would be if our schools simply became 26,000 manila folders.

Most other countries do believe in some form of local regional government, for the very reason that it can be closer to the people concerned than can the capital city. Does anyone really believe that a Secretary of State, were he in charge of all our schools, given all his tremendous powers nowadays, would actually be benign, would generously give all schools several times as much money as they now get, or, indeed, would effectively monitor 26,000 schools? It is easy to forget that local authorities were set up in the first place partly because of the difficulty of keeping an eye on scattered schools.

Some have a hankering to be ruled by the powerful and argue that a national dictator is precisely what we need. Perhaps the escalating use of power is something that should even be learned at school as part of the national curriculum. If so, then the attainment target 'Megalomania' might contain the following ingredients:

Level 1
Gets stroppy with waiters, queries bills automatically.

Level 2
Pushes way into queues, treads on corns.

Level 3
Demands best seats in restaurants, drops coat deliberately so head waiter has to pick it up.

Level 4
Uses loud voice to announce presence or get own way.

Level 5
Leaps on to platform or raised position and orders people around.

Level 6
Stands on roof of building with megaphone to announce decisions.

Level 7
Purchases throne and four large mirrors for own room.

Level 8
Goes round on stilts carrying bullwhip

Level 9
Wears crown, uses royal 'we', offers ring for people to kiss.

Level 10
Salivates, bawls at everybody irrespective of behaviour or rank, has permanently rotating eyeballs.

No problem about standard attainment tasks. Lift-off into megalomaniac lunacy seems to occur at about level 6, so key stage 4 SATs could have items like: take eight counters, push two up each nostril and two in each ear and then say: 'All in a straight line now, I'm in charge. You've all just opted out.'

Times Educational Supplement 22.3.91

In danger of being knocked senseless

'Royalty, squire? I'll tell you all about Royalty. When they're not on a skiing holiday they're swanning around in some castle with a dozen flunkeys in ridiculous fancy dress queuing up to tie their shoelaces. Either that or they're stuffing themselves with sturgeon vol-au-vents and quail pâté.

'And what about the Prince Charles then? Talk to his plants? Listen pal, I can tell you this for a fact. He's given 'em all Christian names. Straight up. Into his greenhouse every day and it's 'Morning Algernon' or 'Pip pip, Laetitia'. Royalty? Bloody daft lot if you ask me.'

Forgive me. I do not actually believe any of these things about Royalty. In fact, I like Prince Charles because he seems genuinely to care about people, but I thought that if he can engage in a bit of common sense theorising about education, why can't I do the same about Royalty? That is the trouble with a Prince Charles common man speech. It sprays common sense buckshot over so many targets it can mean whatever you want.

You like teachers? No problem. Prince Charles said that teachers were suffering from innovation fatigue, poor pay and lack of resources. You dislike teachers? No problem. Prince Charles said that standards of handwriting, spelling and numeracy were too low. It is hardly surprising, therefore, that Kenneth Clarke commended him for talking a lot of common sense, and that Jack Straw described the same speech as a powerful indictment of the Government's policies.

Like everyone else on this planet I believe that common sense, the intuitive practical understanding of every day affairs, is a good thing and that I personally am especially well endowed with it. The trouble with common sense theorising, however, is that it is often wrong. Prejudices and misconceptions can be collectively reinforced to the point where they become accepted truths.

Ask Prince Charles about standards of maths among primary-school children in the 1980s and he will tell you that they went down. Yet the test data on 11-year-olds collected by the Assessment of Performance Unit during the decade showed that in four out of five areas tested (geometry, algebra, measures and probability/statistics) standards actually went up. When he

31

once berated state schools for poor standards of literacy because he had to correct the grammar and spelling of his office staff, it turned out that they had all been privately educated.

Quiz people about those who leave school without a single written qualification and they will no doubt quote the 40 per cent figure commonly given. Yet this is based on an oft repeated 1960s assumption that if the top 20 per cent did O-level, and the next 40 per cent took CSE, that would leave a further 40 per cent with nothing. The true position now is that 90 per cent of pupils obtain a graded GCSE. It is not only Prince Charles who has been commended for his common sense in the past few weeks. The Prime Minister, in his celebrated interview with Sue Lawley, complained that he was surrounded by people with arms full of qualifications who were absolutely useless and had no common sense at all. Since he is surrounded by people like Kenneth Baker and Kenneth Clarke I can only congratulate him on his judgement.

Sadly I suspect John Major's dismissal of formal qualifications will haunt him from now to the end of time. This is a pity, as he seems to be a capable man who succeeded the hard way and could be relaxed about others who have worked equally hard at acquiring formally accredited expertise. I am sure he did not intend it, but his words seemed to reflect that Neanderthal contempt for the intellectual and the professional (hence the scorn for proper training for teachers), which is manifest in some quarters of the Government.

A world dominated by common sense without expertise would be a disaster, but perhaps we can legitimise it academically. I offer, therefore, this finals paper for a degree-level award for good chaps everywhere.

Times Educational Supplement 3.5.91

UNIVERSITY OF LIFE School of Hard Knocks
BA Honours in Good Chapmanship

Paper 3: Common Sense

Answer any three questions, unless your shrewd human judgement tells you otherwise, in which case answer all the questions, or none of them.

1.   Perform a triple bypass heart operation entirely by using common sense. You must not consult a book.

2.   Be a good chap and extract four wisdom teeth from the terrified patient bound and gagged in the corner of the examination room. Fill any decayed teeth you see only if you feel it would be sensible.

3.   You will be taken to a site where a suspension bridge has fallen into a river. Using your shrewd human judgements on such matters, rebuild it.

4.   Prepare a term's work for 30 15 year-olds, half of whom cannot be controlled by 500 extra police at football matches on Saturday afternoons, and all of whom would prefer not to be in school. Then teach it.

5.   A dangerous psychopath will be brought to you. Devise a course of treatment for him which starts off with you saying: 'Come on now, old chap, let's not be silly about this'.

6.   Using matchsticks, plan the economy for the next five years, remembering to say, 'Economists, guv? If you laid 'em all end to end they wouldn't reach a conclusion'.

7.   Using common sense and your Meccano set build a computer which will control all the flights from Heathrow. Devise a sensible strategy for explaining crashes to bereaved relatives, solicitors and insurance companies.

At the conclusion of the examination take your paper to the invigilator who will tear it up and throw it into the waste bin. (Well, this is the School of Hard Knocks, remember).

Maddened by the money men

It's been a bit quiet here in the Mad Curriculum Disease isolation ward recently. There are three teachers of seven-year-olds who sing the 1960s hit 'Little Boxes' over and over again in close Beverley Sisters type harmony, but even they might be released now that the last few digits have been entered in the SAT sheets.

Kenneth Baker was wheeled in the other day after his address to the Police Federation, muttering extracts from his speech about the crime rates going up by a million trillion per cent, but the police were still doing a grand job. As they strapped him into his strait-jacket I told him to remember what he used to say about the national curriculum. It was not a strait-jacket, but rather a creative framework.

So basically it's just me and the ministers sitting round here nowadays, me strapped into my canvas NHS creative framework, whistling mindlessly 'I Got Those Ole Form Fillin' Blues', they pinioned by their privatised fur-lined creative frameworks, chuckling like happy half-wits and dreaming up more mad ideas for their election manifesto.

I hobbled over to the private Beyond Redemption ward to see these cheerful loons last week, hoping to pick up whatever was the latest wheeze. It was a bit difficult trying to pour a pint of lager down Kenneth Clarke's throat with my arms tied round me, so I did spill a bit of it over his creative framework, but I discovered that they now want to hand over responsibility for auditing the running of schools to firms of accountants from the City.

This sort of notion is rooted in a deep dislike of HM Inspectorate, partly because they belong to Her Majesty and not to politicians, and partly because in their last few annual reports they have been critical of the effects that poor resourcing has had on children's education. Yet when HMI was set up more than 150 years ago the critical value-for-money scrutiny of schools was a central precept, given that someone had to keep an eye on local tricksters who might try to make off with the public funds that were beginning to be made available.

Like most people who work in education I sometimes agree and sometimes disagree with what HMI says and reports. It is true that some of its reports have been through so many drafting and editing processes that they are written in that rather bland 'on the one hand, on the other hand' style which has led people to long for a one-armed inspector.

On the other hand, as they say, it was in the primary survey of the late 1970s that the inspectors pointed out that in only one class in 10 were young children getting a decent science programme. There was plenty of tadpoles and sticky buds, but not much physical science or experimental work. This has led to a distinct improvement over the years and a central place for topics like energy, and activities such as the testing of hypotheses, being found in the national curriculum. In fact, the widespread discussion of the HMI paper on a science curriculum for five to 16 year-olds was an important preparation for the national curriculum.

Despite a good track record there is still a strong desire on the right-wing of the Government to abolish or diminish the independence of HMI. Yet another enquiry, the latest in a long line going back to one done by a bigwig in Marks and Spencer a few years ago, is in process. Funny, isn't it? Nobody ever asks you and me to do a quick appraisal of the biscuit factory, or someone's new line in Y-fronts, yet outsiders are assumed to have superior insights to insiders where education is concerned.

New HMI appointments have been frozen, HMI conferences cancelled at short notice. I received details of a conference one day and notification of its cancellation three days later, surely a British all-comers' record. The post of senior chief inspector was not filled when Eric Bolton announced his retirement, and there are many speculations about who, if anyone, will succeed him. A stockbroker? Gazza? Richard Branson perhaps, who has already been in charge of litter and condoms?

What is chilling about the proposal to bring in firms of City accountants is not so much the idea of an external auditor, that is standard practice in many fields, but the suggestion made in one newspaper report that these accountants might stray over into such matters as curriculum, special education needs and teaching methods. 'You cannot be serious,' I screamed at ministers in my best John McEnroe voice, leading to another couple of days in solitary.

Can you imagine your school being driven by an accountant's view of these things? A dreary, monochrome, balance-sheet, profit-and-loss, performance-indicator, instrumental, top-sliced, myopic, cash-dominated perspective on some poor beggar with learning difficulties? Or ace teachers held in check by an albatross in a grey suit? Give me an HMI in a grey suit any day.

What is more, I don't want to hear any guff about what nice chaps accountants are, and how imaginative, resourceful and kind to animals they can be. Of course most accountants are splendid human beings, but they should not be let within several light years of such professional issues as teaching strategies and special educational needs. If anyone may have a go at these crucial professional matters, however, then I hereby claim the reciprocal right to build suspension bridges, perform liver transplants and fly jumbo jets.

They're letting us all out tomorrow. The ministers are off to publish their manifesto. It should be good — all teachers to wear roller skates when teaching, salaries to be paid in Mars bars, headships for anyone who can play the South American nose flute, statutory requirement to stand on your head and whistle 'Rule Britannia' during assembly — who knows what other belters the little tinkers dreamed up while lurching around in their creative frameworks in the Beyond Redemption private ward.

Me? I think I'll stay in the NHS Mad Curriculum Disease isolation ward as a voluntary patient. It could be the safest and sanest place to be, till the accountants come to cost my stay — or perform a lobotomy.

Times Educational Supplement 12.7.91

What to do with Teacher this summer

You know those features on 'What to do with your children this summer' that fill the newspapers at the end of July, telling you how to keep your urchins out of your hair by sending them off to a theme park, urging them to visit long-lost relatives, or persuading them to collect jam jars, well I have always wanted to write one for teachers.

What set me thinking was reading that Powergen had donated rulers to a school. This raised some intriguing questions. Why rulers? Was it a hangover from pre-privatisation days, before the flash logos and lavish television advertising campaigns telling us that electricity makes light bulbs light up?

Incidentally, these ads always seemed to me a most valuable, if expensive, contribution to national curriculum science, about level one-ish of Attainment Target 11. 'Electricity and magnetism', when science still had 17 of them to play with, before they were cut down to five. They were second in value only to the water boards telling us that water comes from rain. What these industrial giants have done for level one of the national curriculum is nobody's business, but I digress.

Does this ill-advised disposal of rulers mean that all our electricity bills will now arrive with wiggly lines instead of straight ones? Or was it just that Powergen had a fairly traditional idea of what schools do nowadays, so the choice was between rulers or slates? I really feel deprived not knowing the answer to all these intriguing questions. After all, if schools are expected to be entrepreneurial, then we should be given a few clues to the thinking in industrial circles nowadays, just in case someone feels disposed to write to a few firms, hoping to pick up a bit of modest sponsorship or even some cash.

This, therefore, is the first item in my 'What teachers can do to while away the summer break' proposals. Try speculating what different firms might produce for you if you wrote and asked. Could anyone be disposing of a rod, pole or perch? A few bushels of slide rules maybe? The odd cane? So get writing those letters. In the immortal words of one of the more cerebral giants of sport, when asked why, after a goal famine, he had scored a hat-trick, 'As the boss told me, like, if you don't buy a raffle ticket you won't win a prize', which probably said it all.

The next funsy possibility one balmy evening during August is to pen your application for the vacant post of chief executive of the National Curriculum Council. Duncan Graham, who is leaving, always had the courage to speak his mind, but the Secretary of State acquired over 400 extra powers under the 1988 Education Act, so, if you are appointed, there is a fair chance that your advice will be ignored and that you will then be blamed for whatever goes wrong.

If you really want the job then choose your words carefully. Something like, 'Dear Minister, I promise to be a suggestible wimp with an inexhaustible appetite for saying, 'You're absolutely right' and 'I couldn't agree more', looking for an outlet for my long-standing and deeply rooted masochistic tendencies. Yours sincerely, A Lapdog,' should do the trick.

Another one for Torquay beach (or Benidorm beach for that matter, depending where you are on the salary scale — Benidorm if you're at the bottom, Torquay if you're at the top) is to design a historical theme park for the year 2091 A hundred years from now there will no doubt be just as much appetitie for visiting heritage centres as there is today, so plan a 2091 AD theme park which includes a 100-year-old school.

Just imagine what citizens might do in such a 21st-century fun park to relive 1991. They could watch the water trickling down the wall from the leaking roof (It must have been grim in Elizabethan times, Esmerelda, aren't you glad you go to school now?); give several SATs to their hapless seven-year-old (Ho ho ho, they didn't do *that* sort of thing did they? How quaint!); or tick endless boxes in little grids (Weren't they primitive in those days? How did they ever find time to teach, for goodness' sake?).

An animated model of Kenneth Clarke could sit in a glass case by the entrance, laughing incessantly at the whole thing, like the laughing man at Blackpool Pleasure Beach.

When you are really desperate try concocting one of those automated records of achievement. In order to cut down the enormous amount of labour involved in writing numerous profiles, some firms have come up with packages designed to take the elbow grease out of report writing. You are given a template and you simply fill in all the gaps, to make it look like a personalised, bespoke, carefully thought out and immensely shrewd assessment, as, for example, in the comment: 'I am... (pleased/sorry) to say that... (name of pupil) has spent much of this year behaving in a(n)... manner'.

There are countless possibilities here for a fertile imagination. Don't be satisfied with such orthodoxy as 'I am pleased to say that Fiona has spent much of this year behaving in an exemplary manner', or 'I am sorry to say that Darren has spent much of this year behaving in an antisocial manner'.

Why not go the whole hog and let rip with, 'I am in ecstasy, nay delirious, to say that Shane, or 'loopy drawers', El Spasmo', 'Thickie Thornton', or 'Psycho III', as I and the rest of the class prefer to call him, has spent much of this year behaving in a 'My goodness, this certainly tells you a lot about his parents, doesn't it, the poor, luckless beggar' manner'?

When you have finished this exercise you can move on to a similar one for teacher appraisal, with such outlines as, 'Your class management reminds me of... and your lesson preparation is best described as...', inviting responses like, 'Your class management reminds me of the House of Commons/the Inquisition, and your lesson preparation is best described as invisible/effortless/so pedantic it makes DES circulars look like the chariot race in *Ben Hur*'.

Have a good summer.

Times Educational Supplement 26.7.91

Don't let chaos loose in class

Recently, *The Independent* has trailed what is said to be a possible feature in the next Conservative election manifesto; namely, that teacher training might be dispensed with and the next generation of recruits simply sent out into schools to pick up what is necessary by osmosis — exactly as happened in the nineteenth century. I have no idea whether this daft idea is is a runner or not, but nowadays nothing in education would surprise me. Monday's crazy horse becomes Tuesday's Education Act and Wednesday's chaos.

I work in a university school of education and it concerns me a great deal therefore, when I read some of the ill-informed and inaccurate assertions made about teacher training, often by people whose knowledge of the subject is about as intimate as my familiarity with the dark side of the planet Pluto.

Much of the negative imagery has been fashioned by right-wing pressure groups such as the Centre for Policy Studies and Adam Smith Institute. Some of these rantings have then been picked up quite uncritically by newspaper leader writers, even when the points made by pressure groups are demonstrably wrong.

I still cannot work out why so many leaders in national newspapers, including *The Independent* and *The Guardian,* are consistently negative about state schools generally and teachers and teacher training in particular. I suspect they are written by the same retired colonel moonlighting around the whole of Fleet Street and Wapping.

Several myths are perpetuated. The first is that teacher trainers are mainly Marxists peddling out-of-date doctrines to gullible trainees, or fanatical supporters of a single approach to teaching. Most of the ones I know are rather straight, did not even wear beads in the Sixties, and follow the family motto, 'slightly middle of centre'.

Another fantasy put about is that training is a barrier to recruitment and competence. This is an especially dotty proposition. In the Seventies and Eighties it was possible for graduates in maths and science to enter teaching without taking a training course. Each year, however, 2,000 or more would opt for a course, despite the exemption, and only 100 or so would go straight in.

In the Sixties, when it was still possible to compare trained and untrained entrants to the profession, Mildred Collins conducted a study of two matched groups of graduate entrants, one trained, the other not. The untrained group received lower ratings from heads, were absent more often, were less likely to read professional journals and keep up-to-date, were more likely to fail their probationary year, and were more likely to quit teaching altogether — not exactly a success story.

Even more astonishing is the proposal to abolish the BEd. This would rob the profession of thousands of excellent primary teachers. It is devilishly difficult to cover the nine subjects of the national curriculum in a one year course. Over four years all subjects, including science and technology — inadequately dealt with years ago, when courses were shorter — can be given reasonable time and practical experience.

Furthermore, to abolish the secondary BEd would be to lose thousands of good recruits in vital subjects such as science, technology, mathematics and physical education. Anyone who argues that if such students did a degree first, they would automatically enter teaching has no idea of the employment patterns of graduates today. Many would take their degree and go and work in the City, in banking or insurance instead. There would be a huge net loss and severe future recruitment problems.

Worse still is the chaos that would ensue if thousands of trainees were simply turned loose, inadequately prepared, on schools that are themselves often struggling to implement government policies. There would eventually be an outcry from parents, once they realised what had happened. It would be a restoration of the disastrous training practices of the nineteenth century which, after numerous scandals, were replaced by a properly constituted training procedure. I have seen teacher training in several European countries, Asia and North America. What we have in Britain, while not perfect, is far better than what is done in most countries. Good teacher training today is essentially practical and involves a close partnership between trainers and teachers in schools, each with an important part to play.

Many primary teachers can give excellent on-the-job guidance, but would readily admit they have little self-confidence in science and technology. At Exeter our undergraduates and postgraduates are trained by tutors who have successful primary teaching experience and higher degrees in science, so they can speak or demonstrate with authority on scientific and educational matters. Her Majesty's Inspectorate reports are largely positive, and a team of senior inspectors, after a visit to my own department, said they had seen some of the best teaching they had ever witnessed.

I do not know whether or not the Government has radical plans to restore nineteenth-century training practice for other professions, but if there is any likelihood of some ill-prepared, scalpel-wielding novice embarking on a random search for my appendix, I would appreciate due notice.

Independent 4.4.91

Chapter 3

Crisis Management

Dirty tricks that bring in filthy lucre

Ladies and gentlemen, welcome to the first staff meeting since we opted out and became Upper Swinesville Elite College of Secondary Education. As you know there was a two-thirds to one-third majority among parents on the second ballot in favour of opting out. I shall never forget that emotional moment last year when the chairman of governors announced the results of the historic vote: parents in favour of opting out, 2; parents against, 1; down at the pub, 368; watching *East Enders,* 2,137.

I should like, in this my first report as chief executive, to explain to you some decisions that I have made in consultation with the managing director, as the former chairman of governors is now known. We intend to put Upper Swinesville on the map as the trendsetter among grant-maintained schools. Before long the world will be beating a path to our door to see how opting out should be done.

Let me first of all bring you up to date on what has been happening so far. You will be pleased to hear that the Government has announced a new building grant scheme for opted-out schools. There are two units, a Bribe, which is worth £100,000, and a Backhander, which is £25,000. We have been granted six Bribes and three Backhanders, so we shall have £675,000 for school building projects.

In order to secure this Government money we had to agree to certain conditions. The main one was that every pupil has to wear a grey suit. Now I know that some of you feel the girls in particular look silly, but it is a small price to pay for all the money we shall be getting.

I should like to announce the results of the competition held by the school governors, or board of directors as they are now known. You will remember that staff were asked to propose a new school motto. Well I am pleased to say, with all due modesty, that the winner was my own crisp suggestion of 'Up yours, Swinesville LEA'.

Next the question of recruitment of new pupils. The board has decided to go for an aggressive, hard-hitting strategy. You may have heard the commercials on local radio stations with the punchline, 'Come to Upper Swinesville Elite College. All other schools are scum'. We thought this had bite and would reinforce the leaflet we have been distributing round primary schools entitled. 'Only plonkers go to Lower Swinesville Comp'.

The board has drawn up a checklist for staff to use when interviewing potential parents. Each characteristic is awarded a plus or a minus score. The plus scores include 'Father wearing grey suit' (plus five), 'Mother wearing grey suit' (plus 10), 'Look filthy rich' (plus 20) 'Look filthy rich and gullible' (offer unconditional place).

The minus scores are 'Asks awkward questions' (minus five), 'unlikely to have bred someone who can knock up decent GCSE grades and shove us up the test score league table' (minus 10), 'Unwilling to run raffles' (minus 20), and 'Not members of golf club' (reject outright).

You will know that the Government is seeking to change the teachers' pay scales to give opted-out schools like ourselves the maximum freedom to offer whatever salaries the market decrees. The board has decided to introduce a new scheme of performance-related pay, in accordance with Government policy, and I should like to describe the details of this.

In future teachers will be paid a certain number of flat-rate payments and then additional sums according to performance criteria. The flat-rate payments to all staff include a personal chalk allowance (£10) and a grey suit allowance (£50).

The £50 will allow you to buy a new grey suit every year in the Xmas, New Year, spring, Easter, early, mid or late summer, autumn or winter sale at the managing director's SupaSwish Clothing Mart. In response to your query, Mr Hardcastle, about whether staff can save up for three or four year and then purchase something less likely to disintegrate at the cleaners, I can only say that tasteless jokes like that will do you no good in the forthcoming salary negotiations.

The salary performance criteria have been carefully worked out by myself and the board. They will soon be the envy of the world and are likely to be copied throughout the land, just you wait and see. Each criterion has been conceived as a brand new unit of measurement, with a score from one to five, depending on how highly you are rated. Bonus payments will then be paid according to your overall score.

Perhaps I can illustrate how this will work with a few specific examples from those who have scored highly on the various performance criteria. You will be pleased to hear, Mrs Jenkins, that on the first criterion 'Knocking the opposition' for which the unit is a 'Tebbit', you scored a maximum of five Tebbits for writing to the *Swinesville Gazette* and suggesting that Lower

Swinesville comprehensive, since it is unable to fill its four teaching vacancies, will soon be a good example of the classless society.

On the other hand, I am sorry to say that Mr Hardcastle, who was overheard arguing that Lower Swinesville had a very good science department, has come down heavily on the second criterion, which is 'Appeasement'. Each unit here means a salary debit, and I'm afraid you lost five MacGregors for that careless moment Mr Hardcastle.

Criterion three is called 'Combative rudeness' and we were extremely impressed with your performance here Miss Fothergill. The two best instances were when you called the Swinesville chief education officer 'an overpaid bureaucratic nerd' and when you rejected the parent applicant whom you described as 'a thick navvy'. Top score to you for those and other gems, Miss Fothergill, of five Clarkes.

Finally the fourth performance criterion 'Obsequiousness'. For overall crawling there was no one to match the man who showed himself to be in a class of his own. So you can get off you knees now, Mr Bidgood, as my shoes have a lovely shine. You fully deserve your score of five Bakers, and I call on the managing director to present you with this year's Golden Oildrum.

Times Educational Supplement 14.12.90

A Christmas tale

It was Christmas Eve, a bit of a rum time for a governors' meeting, but then in Snowland absolutely everything happened on Christmas Eve.

May I call the meeting to order please?' Santa boomed, 'I promised Mrs Claus I'd pop home for a quick sandwich before I set off on my world-wide delivery round.'

'Why don't you deliver the National Curriculum while you're about it?' muttered Mr Hardcastle, the embittered teacher governor, who felt duty bound to make rude comments about Kenneth Baker's reforms at every governors' meeting.

The assorted collection of what constituted the Snowland School governing body came slowly to order. Outside in the bleak early evening Santa's reindeer whinnied plaintively, or whatever reindeer do when they're standing restlessly in front of a fully laden sledge. There were Donner and Blitzen, Dancer and Prancer, and, since two of the reindeer were suffering from leg injuries, Wally and Plonker, the two school inspectors who had agreed to help out.

'Item 1, apologies. There are no apologies,' Santa began. 'Item 2, may I sign the minutes of our meeting last Christmas Eve? Fine. Item 3, matters arising. Yes, Mrs Fitzwarren?'

Mrs Fitzwarren loved the formality of committee meetings. Long service on the Snowland District Council had taught her every technical committee term in the book. There was nothing she enjoyed more than explaining to the parent governors whether amendments had to be voted on before substantive motions.

'I should like to ask the Headmaster, if I may, through the Chair, to...'

'Why not ask him through your mouth like everybody else?' interjected the uncouth Mr Hardcastle.

Mrs Fitzwaren fixed him with that acetylene torch glare of hers that had melted every igloo in Snowland 'I should be grateful if the Headmaster could bring us up to date on the present state of LMS,' she continued.

'The LMS?' cried Colonel Ffrenchly Fforbes, springing upright and then having to twiddle one of the knobs of his life-support machine. 'I thought that was closed down years ago when they nationalised the railways.'

46

No one knew why the old dodderer was still on the governing body. He had been nominated by the local authority years ago because he was rumoured to be the last survivor of the Light Brigade. Every third or fourth topic on the agenda he would suddenly call out, 'Charge!' and yet another item would be added to the parents' growing bill. Still, it solved the problem of what and what not to charge parents for under the more diffuse sections of the 1988 Education Act.

'Look, we must get a move on,' Santa murmured apologetically 'We've yet to hear the Headmaster's report on the latest subject in the National Curriculum.'

'Thank you, Mr Chairman,' said the Headmaster, drawing himself up to his full height of two foot six. There was never any problem casting the part of Dopey in the school's annual production of *Snow White and the Seven Dwarfs*.

'The latest subject in the National Curriculum is 'snow'. There are, you will be interested to hear, only three attainment targets compared with the 17 in science and the 14 in maths, so this is quite a relief. Attainment target 1 is 'ice', number 2 is 'hail' and number 3 is 'slush'. By Level 2, which the average seven-year-old should achieve, children should be able to recognise a snowflake. By Level 4, which the average 11-year-old should reach, they should be able to construct a decent snowball.'

'What about assessment, through you, of course, Mr Chairman?' asked Mrs Fitzwarren smugly, anxious to show off that she knew such a thing existed.

'Ah that's an excellent question,' the Headmaster oiled, well aware that extra salary points for senior staff were now determined by the governors. 'There will be a standard assessment task based on the interdisciplinary theme 'snow across the curriculum'. Children will be expected, by Level 6, to construct an igloo, measure it, weigh it, write a poem about it and then pole vault over it.' The Headmaster droned on interminably about levels, standard assessment tasks, and cross curricular themes.

'What about profile components?' demanded Mrs Fitzwarren imperiously, spitting out more of her National Curriculum dictionary.

Santa stared blankly out into the chilly night, wondering why he had allowed himself to be dragooned firstly into standing as a parent governor and then into becoming Chairman. He recalled the story about Peter Sellers being seated, on one occasion, in a restaurant next to a table of pretentious and noisy fellow diners, and then, in sheer anger and frustration, leaping on to his chair and bawling out at the top of his voice, 'American Cream Ices'.

Santa resisted the temptation to do the same. Instead he contented himself with longing wistfully for the days when governors met for a mince pie and a glass of grog, solely to confirm that the next governors' meeting would again be held on Christmas Eve.

Home and School, Winter Issue 1990

Paper piles that reduce us all to pulp

Over the years there have been many fads and phases in educational management. Some have stressed the need for written objectives, others the charisma of a leader. In recent times there has been emphasis on systems and structures, occasionally sporting titles like the 'cybernetics' model.

As I recall, the Cybermen in *Dr Who* were machine-like creatures who wandered along with the sort of fixed, blank expression most of us would wear if we had to conduct our daily business with a 1950s vacuum cleaner wrapped round our upper body. At its worst, unmitigated by human warmth, any system which sees children and teachers as mere boxes, to be filled with 'inputs' in order to obtain 'outputs', will produce equally blank uniformity.

It is too easy, however, to attack an extreme version of the systems approach, and then pretend that there can be no place for any organised or rationally-based management in such an essentially human activity as education. That would be complete nonsense. Good management sets up the conditions in which ingenuity can flourish, and this can involve deliberate action according to well-founded and agreed principles.

What concerns me is not the imminent hijacking of educational management by a gang of marauding Cybermen, but rather the way in which the servants of the systematic approach can become its masters. I have been looking at one of the well-established trends, Management by Paper, set to dominate the 1990s as it did the late 1980s, and it does not offer a happy prospect.

I have nothing against paper, you understand. I actually love it, wrap things in it, write on it, read what's written on it by others. Whenever I open a new pack of paper I feel a huge sense of achievement, only let down by the need to make just one more cup of tea before writing on it.

It is even the central piece of my favourite game, Bureaucratic Basketball, the rules of which are simple: site the waste-paper basket at the far end of the room, screw up each unwanted piece of A4 into a tight ball and see how many you can land in the basket. At 15ft or so, 5 out of 10 is sound, 7 out of 10 is good, 9 out of 10 is brilliant. If you can score 10 out of 10 with your back to the basket, using the hook shot over your shoulder, then you must work in education.

As a servant of the human race, paper is fine, but as a master it takes on a tyrannical life of its own. I once acted as an external examiner at a college. After the final meeting to decide the results I received a postcard from one of the big cheeses at the college, renowned for his addiction to Management by Paper. Headed 'External Examiners' it read: 'The college would like to thank you for acting as external examiner this year and for the conscientious way in which you carried out your duties'.

I was immediately intrigued. The non-aligned date and the plural 'Examiners' in the heading suggested that this was standard annual letter. Did that mean everyone got it, in which case what about the external examiner I once heard of who lost half the scripts, or the one who caught the train to the wrong college because he was doing so much examining he no longer knew where he was; or even the one who fell asleep in the meeting? Had they examined at that college would they all have qualified for the big cheese's same congratulatory postcard?

Or did he have other standard versions in his vast collection of templates? Perhaps there was, in one of his many filing cabinets, a 'congratulations on actually turning up this year' or 'sincere gratitude for not snoring when you nodded off' outline.

One of the most interesting fields when studying Management by Paper is the use of the memo. A written memo is, of course, a very valuable tool, especially when several people need to be in the know, or when a permanent record of a transaction is needed. However, memos can take on a life of their own. They are even capable of reproduction.

Scientists do not yet fully understand exactly how two memos actually mate, but the conditions and effects are well documented. Indeed it is possible to perform one's own experiment to study the process. Address the first memo to Donald Duck, but with a copy to Mickey Mouse. It should be slightly acrimonious with a hint that Mickey Mouse *and unnamed others,* for this is a crucial ingredient if mating is to take place, may be implicated.

By return of post Donald Duck will reply angrily, with the adult equivalent of a threat to take his ball home. This memo will have automatically been copied to Mickey Mouse, as he was on the first list, but there will be a curt footnote saying, 'Out of common courtesy I have copied this memo to Goofy and Pluto, who have been unfairly put under suspicion by your note'. The phrase 'common courtesy' is also necessary for reproduction to take place, as it hints that others are discourteous and also a bit common.

At this point the progenitor can sit back and watch the dynasty grow. Hurt memos from Goofy and Pluto, pointing out that their dad is bigger than your dad, fly towards Donald Duck, with a copy to Mickey Mouse, but also to Bugs Bunny, Elmer Fudd, Woody Woodpecker and any other Loony Tunes who might be sympathetic or influential. Whole forests bite the dust as two memos beget millions, and all because someone first used the anonymity of paper as a substitute for courage, and then became the victim and slave of it.

The worst feature of Management by Paper is the belief that paper is not merely the lubricant for, or record of action, but is itself the action. It is akin to that enormous feeling of achievement we have when we *buy* a book and feel we have read it. Producing a policy statement may be an important precursor to solving a problem or clarifying confusion, but it is no substitute for intelligent action itself.

Two final thoughts occur to me. One is that, with electronic mailing and other information technology widely available, some institutions already have Management by InfoTech, the natural successor to Management by Paper.

The other is the comment from a Swede I met recently who has seen off the Cybermen. He asked: 'Why are you burying schools under thousands of sheets of paper with your national curriculum? We are going in the opposite direction. We have given them about 15 pages of outline and challenged them to get on with it'. I love you, my sensible friend.

Times Educational Supplement 11.1.91

How vouchers could privatise schools

There was considerable surprise in the world of education when Margaret Thatcher revived, once more, the prospect of educational vouchers.

The proposal, to offer parents a voucher equivalent to the cost of a child's education which could be cashed either at a local school or at another of their choice, enjoyed a brief spell in the limelight about five years ago. At that time Sir Keith Joseph said he was 'intellectually attracted' to the idea.

The notion of a voucher began in the United States, in particular in a place called Alum Rock, where it was seen as a bit of a left-wing wheeze for giving more muscle to less wealthy parents. It crossed the Atlantic and became a right-wing cause for free marketeers keen to introduce more competition into what they saw as a monopoly.

Until the Conservative Party conference it seemed to have disappeared from the political agenda, Sir Keith having eventually rejected the idea.

Teachers' leaders were particularly concerned about parents moving children from school to school and the instability this might cause. They imagined lorries carting temporary buildings from unpopular school to popular school, only to find that the popular school had now become overcrowded and hence unpopular, so the huts and teachers would have to move camp again. There were jokes about jobless teachers hanging around motorway service stations hitching a ride on a passing school.

Since that time, apart from a brief hint a couple of years ago that students in higher education might be given vouchers to spend at the university or polytechnic of their choice, the proposal has lain quietly buried, with just an occasional mention by small pressure groups.

Mrs Thatcher's announcement that there might be a revival of the scheme was either, therefore, a piece of mischievousness, the sort of thing someone might do at the end of a boring week just to watch everyone scuttle round trying to guess what it meant, or, much more likely, a message that vouchers were under active consideration.

If this is so, then it could represent the most spectacular step towards privatisation of a public service yet conceived, and the implications for other public services could be enormous.

The 1988 Education Act introduced the right to 'open enrolment', that is the entitlement of parents to send their children to the school of their choice, unless that school could be proved to be as full as it had been a decade earlier, when pupil numbers were at their height nationally. In addition, schools were to be funded, not according to some historical precedent, but on a per capita basis depending on the number of pupils on the roll.

The same happened to universities and polytechnics. The message was clear: the more pupils, the more cash. It looked like a clever voucher scheme without the vouchers and accompanying bureaucracy.

There appear to be only two explanations for the Prime Minister's new interest in vouchers. The first would be for political reasons. Although parents have an entitlement under open enrolment, the voucher in their hand would have the appearance of a gift from a customer-supportive government wanting to give power and choice to the consumer.

There is a problem about this, however. When vouchers were last discussed, one reason for a waning of enthusiasm was a hint from a Conservative-controlled local authority, which had looked into it, that the administrative costs could be £1m. With more than 100 local authorities, vouchers would, at £100m, be an expensive gimmick, especially as they would benefit parents no more than the 1988 Education Act. If a school is genuinely full, then it is full, and voucher-waving parents will be shown the door. However, schools willing to raise extra cash by taking even more pupils can take the initiative now — under formula funding they would get the money.

But it is the second, and more likely, motive which takes the breath away. It seems highly probable that the Prime Minister would like parents to be able to cash their vouchers at an independent or private school. The price of such a move would be astronomical. Currently, nearly 8 per cent of pupils attend schools in the private sector.

The average cost of educating our eight million schoolchildren varies from region to region and from primary to secondary, but a cautious estimate would be around £1,200 per capita per annum. Multiply that by the number of children who would use their voucher in the private sector, add the £100m for administration, and the cost would be £870m.

What appeared to be a throwaway remark, therefore, might represent a willingness to consider shunting over some £750m of public money into the private sector of education. I should not myself be at all surprised.

Independent 18.10.90

Spitting image of a predatory spiv

If there is one major pitfall for the unwary it is the possibility of handing over hard-earned cash to some of the fly-by-nights passing themselves off as experts and consultants in such fields as evaluation, fundraising and marketing. The genuine firms and individuals can indeed help schools improve their finances or sharpen up their presentation of themselves, but some of the spivs and predators one encounters nowadays could not be trusted with anything as important as a fish and chip shop, let alone a school.

Many schools have improved their standing with the public or made themselves more efficient without voting a penny piece to an outside firm. Judicious application of common sense and a bit of native wit can achieve at least as much as the average consultant would bring, and a great deal more than Easy Peasy Enterprise Inc. or Money For Old Rope Plc. Only the very best are worth parting with cash for.

In any case most consultants and external evaluators use a limited range of standard procedures around which there should be no mystique. The first step is to talk to the natives, on the grounds that many people who work in a place have a shrewd idea of what is going on and what needs to be done. There is, apparently, no shortage of people gullible enough to pay someone to tell them what they already know or could easily find out.

Imagine that you have to appraise the local basket-weaving factory. By chatting to the people who work there you might discover that the foreman has long lunch hours and then rolls in drunk, that the manager spends much of his time in his office and has lost touch with the ordinary worker, and that the flange splinger keeps breaking down.

Now all you have to do is relay this to the board of directors in a glossy report, in which you also suggest a new flange splinger, a fresh image, a relaunch and laying off a quarter of the staff, and you will be hailed as one of the last examples of pure living genius. Either the board knew these things anyway, but needed the authority of an external report so they could act, or they themselves were out of touch. Don't stop to find out. Take the money and run.

Another common device used by marketing consultants is known as USP, the Unique Selling Point. The art here is to find something that the business or school has which gives it an edge over others. The exercise begins with the consultant asking people to assemble a list of the school's features they think are unique, perhaps having its own swimming pool, or being the only school in town with a roof that doesn't leak.

Not all such distinctive features are necessarily useful. Having a higher crime rate or more headlice than any other school, or a caretaker who can juggle with four cans of floor polish, may not readily translate into crisp recruiting slogans — 'Burglary across the curriculum: a new national curriculum cross-curricular theme, level 7 guaranteed', 'Save the nit, come to Swinesville High', 'Juggle with Joe'. I can't see it myself.

Identifying the USP is often a part of a wider strategy known as SWOT. I swear I am not making these things up, by the way. SWOT is an acronym of Strengths, Weaknesses, Opportunities and Threats. A school might identify its close ties with the community as a strength, its shabby buildings as a weakness, the appointment of a new deputy responsible for curriculum as an opportunity and the potential loss of pupils following a rehousing scheme as a threat.

You can see why I said there should be no mystique surrounding all this simple application of commonsense, and why cash need not change hands. You can even make up your own equally valid strategies and acronyms, like Troubles, Openings, Successes and Horrors (TOSH) or Commitments, Rationale, Activities and Problems (CRAP).

Much time is often spent by PR firms on image-making and self-representation. There is, however, a delicate balance between on the one hand never letting the public know what a school is doing and the kind of nauseating image-making proposed by Easy Peasy Enterprises Inc. Some PR firms that have worked mainly in commerce see image-making as essentially competitive and cannot understand schools that want to work harmoniously with their neighbours.

The clear presentation of actuality, rather than the manufacture of dishonest imagery, should be an obligation on all schools. Many have managed to obtain regular space in local newspapers by working closely with journalists and editors, sometimes as a group of schools. Every minute spent publicising the good that happens in a particular school is time well spent on behalf of everyone in education, not just the school concerned. After the substantial negative publicity during the past few months each local effort can help rebuild public confidence.

There is no need for most schools to give any cash at all to external PR firms. The techniques they will use are freely available to anyone with more than 10 brain cells. They can also be learnt, for a fraction of the inflated fees charged by consultancy firms, from numerous books, like the recently published *Public Relations and Marketing for Schools* by Tim Devlin and Brian Knight.

Let me conclude with one major challenge to the image-makers. I am not the world's greatest fan of the mass of attainment targets dreamt up by the several working parties, but if there was one I would have defended to the last ditch it was the proposal by the PE working group that we should try to ensure that children can swim 25 metres by the age of 11. Unfortunately Kenneth Clarke is worried that schools might need cash for swimming lessons, so he has turned it down.

Most children who drown do so a few feet away from safety, rather than in the middle of some raging ocean. Even elementary proficiency such as the ability to swim 10 metres could be the difference between life and death.

If this represents the new caring image of educational policy then I suggest the Department of Education and Science engage Easy Peasy Enterprise Inc. to turn Mr Clarke into Florence Nightingale, but preferably not back again.

Times Educational Supplement 8.3.91

Pressed for constant reassurance

The head of a primary school in a fashionable suburb described to me what has increasingly become a feature of her day. It goes like this.

Knock, Knock, 'Ah, come in Mr and Mrs Bloggs, how nice to see you. It's about spelling, is it? Well, we don't actually have a weekly test, but we do try to correct most spelling mistakes. Yes I did read Mr Clarke's speech and Amanda will be having a spelling test in about a fortnight.'

Ring ring. 'Good morning Mrs Scroggins. Yes it did take a long time to answer the phone, I was trying to find it underneath all these national curriculum papers. It's about your Robert's reading, is it? I have indeed seen the HMI report on reading standards and I can assure you that we use a mixture of methods.

'Well, it depends what you mean by 'real books'. You see, the Bible is a real book. No, I don't mean we teach reading through the Bible that was just and example. Yes, I know you're humanists, but I just wanted to say that we do teach letters. No, we don't just send children to the library to teach themselves to read, it's all exaggerated in the press. Look, let me explain Mrs Scroggins...'

It has become a regular task for primary heads on the phone, at meetings, or in casual conversation, to have to disarm press reports that standards are going to the dogs or that primary schools are awash with loony teachers trying out crazy experiments in the classroom. The recent speech on education by Prince Charles will have been more good news for British Telecom, as anxious parents ring their local school to check out whether what the Prince said is true.

The sheer volume of reports, attacks, claims and counter claims in the mass media, ever since the furore about the reading standards of seven-year-olds and spelling competence last June, has been formidable. It has produced a remarkable schizophrenia among parents.

Public opinion surveys show that about three quarters of parents believe standards are falling, but that more than 80 per cent are satisfied with their own children's teachers. This paradox seems difficult to explain, but the reason is simple. Parents believe that standards must be falling *elsewhere,* not in their own children's primary school.

That is why it is so important for every one of our 21,000 primary schools to continue with, or embark on its 'mission to explain'. Every parents' evening, annual meeting, playground conversation or telephone call during which a parent learns something at first, rather than second, hand, does a valuable service for the whole of education, even if it is in a small two or three-teacher village school.

It is equally important to respond to public debate in schools where parents may not be as persistent in their questions as in the suburban school described above. No one can dispel the myths as effectively as someone closely engaged with and committed to parents' own children, and that is why it is currently one of primary teachers' and heads' most pressing assignments.

Times Educational Supplement 3.5.91

How to cut the cackle and have a laugh

I have gone right off bureaucracy, machinery, meetings — all that parapher-
nalia that should hang around the edge of one's job, but can easily encroach
into the heart of it. Not that I was every happy about any of these, apart from
machinery. Like others who never had a toy train in their youth, I have usually
enjoyed playing with some gleaming new piece of technological wizardry.
But that was before I got my new microcomputer.

Computer instruction manuals are written by people who are mentally
deranged, then translated through Serbo-Croat, Albanian and Coptic and
eventually into what purports to be English. It is normally quite good fun to
translate text through several languages and back into English, especially
when 'Out of sight, out of mind' returns as 'Invisible, insane', but not with
something as vital as a computer manual. It all reminds me of some Japanese
camera instructions I got several years ago. 'Point the subject and shoot.'

Apparently, to make my gleaning new machine work I have to do
something to my *autoexec* file. What on earth is an autoexec? Is is the new
term for one of those highly paid heads of opted out schools who is on
£50,000 a year and a car? Even when I eventually rumbled what it was about,
I still got screen messages saying 'Bad command'. What the hell is a bad
command? As I was writing a book on class management in the primary
school I imagined it must be something like 'Pick up that crisp bag and put
it in your ear,' which seems more of a bad command than whatever I did to
earn the screen reprimand.

I felt like taking a sledge hammer to the whole thing. A couple of days
with this handbook would turn St Francis of Assisi into a foaming psychopath.

Then there is the morning mail. It may just be my imagination but it seems
to be getting ever dafter. I don't mind circulars from the Department of
Education and Science explaining, without irony, that they are going to cut
down the amount of paper they are sending out, nor do I object to the guff
from the armies of 'consultants' selling everything from advice on how to do
the timetable (No thanks, Arthur does it very well already) to 'putting surplus
cash into bricks and mortar', a rum sounding solution to a non-existent

problem. But missives like the circular explaining next year's arrangements for testing seven-year-olds scale new heights of incomprehension.

I once worked in a place where the shredder stood right next to the mail rack. It seemed such a brilliant idea. It was always white hot, as people put the rubbish straight into the shredder without allowing it to enter and destroy the brain.

A few years ago the sociologist and columnist Laurie Taylor wrote about how his mail-opening habits had reversed over time, and I now find myself in exactly the same position. In the past, manila envelopes were opened first, to get the boring bureaucratic stuff and circulars out of the way, then the white envelopes, as they could be quite interesting, and finally the foreign letters with the exotic stamps, in case someone was inviting you to the Bahamas for the weekend. Now you start with the exotic mail, since it contains circulars from the offshore tax haven-based consultants, and finish up with the manila envelope which probably tells you how many thousands have been carved off next year's budget.

Then there is the question of meetings. I don't mind genuine planning meetings, or even the ones where you have to go through exam results and assessments, at whatever tedious length, because these things must be done properly. What sends me up the nearest pole is the windbaggery in those many meetings that only seem to exist to plan the date and time of the next one, but take three hours over it. There seems to be so little you can do when trapped in a room for several hours, apart from asking yourself over and over again 'What on earth am I *doing* here?'

However, there is no point in merely giving up on these things. A former colleague used to fall asleep, as many people do, especially after lunch in warm weather. But he would fall asleep in style, mouth open, head back, the odd raucous snore, none of your subtle dozing.

My own strategy is to cast imaginary films. *On the Waterfront* is an inevitable winner, as you can cast people you don't like as leather-jacketed thugs. The *Carry on* series is also superb, and you can invent your own episode like *Carry on Plonker*. Never do this when chairing a meeting, by the way, I was once well into Wagner's operas in one brain-corroding session I was chairing, when I very nearly called one member Brünnhilde. My best recent fantasy was a sensational all-singing, all dancing version of *Lassie Come Home* starring Kenneth Baker and a pit bull terrier. I won't tell you where the beast's molars ended up.

Another useful defence in meetings is to cheer yourself up by recalling jokes. I was in a meeting a few weeks back in which a newly arrived member was eager for reassurance that his contribution was being valued. He kept asking the chairman for approval of what he had been saying. The meeting coincided with the death of Stanley Mortenson, hero of my childhood, the Blackpool and England footballer who had partnered the fabulous Stanley Matthews in the 1950s. Many affectionate jokes were told about this legendary pair, but the meeting reminded me of one in particular.

One day Stanley Matthews was injured and a promising young lad was brought in to wear the celebrated number 7 shirt. Anxious to show what a good substitute he was, the young lad raced down the right wing, leaving players after player lunging hopelessly in his wake. Three times he darted through the defence and each time sent over an immaculate pin-pointed cross to the head of Stanley Mortenson. Three times Mortenson jackknifed in the air, shouted 'Oooh!' in a loud voice, and headed a superb goal.

At half-time the youth went over to the great man. 'Congratulations on your three goals, Mr Mortenson. Am I doing alright?' he asked anxiously. 'You're doing fine son,' Mortenson replied, 'but just remember one thing. When he sends the ball across to me, Stanley points the lace *towards* the goal.'

Times Educational Supplement 28.6.91

Chapter 4

Life in the classroom

Good teaching follows no easy formula

Was Fagin a good teacher? If the sole criterion were how effectively children had learned what they had been taught, then he would take some beating. But identifying good teachers is not that simple — several other factors are involved.

Good teaching is a highly subjective business. We can all label teachers who taught us at school as effective or ineffective, but our fellow former pupils might not take the same view. I well recall a teacher who seemed at the time to be fairly useless because he kept straying from the syllabus, but in retrospect I can see that much of what I learned was valuable.

Academics have tried for years to identify the elusive qualities of good teachers. Thousands of studies have been undertaken, especially in the United States, but with about as much success as the quest for the philosopher's stone.

One major difficulty lies in establishing criteria. Do you go for exam success? If so, what about the people who teach remedial classes or work with the mentally retarded? And would it mean that teachers who have very bright pupils in their classes would automatically be regarded as brilliant, even if they never did a hand's turn.

On the other hand, if you settle for those who are popular with the children or esteemed by parents or their colleagues, there may be an undue premium on social skills. Similarly, if you send in appraisers to watch lessons, they may be overly impressed by extrovert performers who can put on a good show, rather than quieter practitioners who get results over a long period. Teaching is for stayers rather than sprinters.

Children have no such inhibitions about stating what constitutes good teaching. I once reviewed all the studies I could find of pupils' views on teachers during the last 60 years. It was an astonishingly consistent story. In 1935, 8,000 Birmingham children were asked to order a number of statements about good teachers. Top of their list was the ability to explain things. Nearly 50 years later, I conducted a similar exercise with 12 to 16 year-olds using 32 statements. Firmly at the top of the list was the ability to explain something clearly.

The social psychologist Kurt Lewin argued that children as young as three or four could be acutely sensitive to what constitutes skilful behaviour by adults. Not only do children have a firm view about professional skills like knowing your stuff and being able to explain it, but they are also clear about other aspects.

Children esteem teachers who are slightly strict — rather than overly severe or permissive — scrupulously fair in their use of rewards and punishments, interested in them as individuals, and with a sense of humour which is not based on sarcasm or humiliation.

This somewhat traditional view that the good teacher is firmly in charge can perplex trainees, mostly 19-22 year-olds, who are closer in age to the pupils than their more experienced colleagues and anxious to be seen as friendly. Occasionally, if they have had discipline problems during their teaching practice, they will ask their class to write down what they might have done to improve their teaching. To the trainee's surprise, a large majority of the class will write something like: 'I'm very interested in history (or whatever), but you allowed Dick and Sid to mess about and spoil the lessons'. (Dick and Sid write: 'I'm very interested in history, but you allowed Bill and Fred to mess about...').

Some studies of teaching have looked at specific teachers' skills and tried to relate these to children's learning. I once analysed more than 100 explanations of topics like 'insects' taught to eight and nine year-olds. After each explanation, the class had to identify insects from a sheet full of drawings of various creatures.

The least effective explainers were not always sure themselves of the characteristics of insects, one cheerfully accepting 'spider' and 'centipede' as legitimate examples from the class. The best, on the other hand, were a joy to watch. One built much of his lesson round the question 'Is a bird an insect?' and, by using this as a comparison and looking at real insects, skilfully established criteria such as wings, legs and body shape. Almost every child got full marks on the test.

But what emerges from this kind of study is that the 'good' teachers are almost always different from each other. In the nineteenth century, training institutions were known as 'Normal' schools, on the grounds that there was some single norm that all should strive to copy. Dickens, describing M'Choakumchild in *Hard Times,* wrote: 'He and some 140 schoolmasters had been lately turned at the same time in the same factory, on the same principles, like so many pianoforte legs'.

The quest for a single 'good teacher' stereotype is probably doomed. But if only one style of teaching were approved, schools would have to be staffed by 420,000 clones, with one of them stuffed in a glass case at the Department of Education and Science as an example of the British Standard Teacher. It would be a recipe for turning our children into robots.

The Observer 14.4.91

Appraise yourself

Teachers will be curious to know how they can carry out appraisal for the piddling sum offered by Kenneth 'the Ninja' Clarke. I can now reveal a secret Department of Education and Science plan which offers instant appraisal at a very low cost. For the price of three packets of peanuts I have been developing a self-appraisal kit so that teachers can assess their own performance in the privacy of their own homes — if they can afford one.

The instrument below has been designed according to the latest scientific principles. It is based on a rigorous factor and cluster analysis of thousands of items and conforms to the highest reliability and validity requirements after exhaustive field testing. (Well alright, so I just put down the first thing that came into my head and tried them out on two halfcut teachers down at the local boozer, but what do you expect for 75p?) The test is divided into sections under key headings. You should answer each item and then check your score and prognosis at the end of the test. In each case just tick one response unless you (a) are schizophrenic or (b) have been on a course on assessment recently in which case your brain will be irrevocably scrambled. Answer honestly if you are a teacher with great personal and professional integrity, and dishonestly if you would do anything for promotion, believe in fairies, or have been at the port already.

Lesson Planning

1. HMI are visiting your school and one asks to see your lesson plans. Do you reply:

    a. They are all neatly filed in those six leather-bound files over there

    b. I'm a genius squire. It's all in here (pointing to your head)

    c. I'm a genius squire. It's all in here (pointing to another part of your anatomy)

Recognising Acronyms

2. What does SEAC stand for:

    a. School Examinations and Assessment Council

    b. Standards 'Ere Are Climbing

    c. Squashes Easily All Creativity

3. Which of the following is the odd one out:

    a. SEAC

    b. NCC

    c. BUM

Class Management

4. You find a huge queue has built up at your desk. Do you:

    a. Say, 'Right, go and sit down everybody and I'll just deal with the major problems'

    b. Hope that, with luck, the queue will keep going until the bell

    c. Ask each child what he wants and then send him to the back of the queue for not expressing himself properly

5. You detect some noisy disruption and filthy language from someone at the back of the room. Do you:

    a. Say, 'What on earth is going on here? I will not tolerate that kind of obscene language in my classroom'

    b. Reprimand the culprit for his vile mouth and then send him to the head

    c. Discover it is the head

Classroom Skills

6. You are doing electrical circuits with your class and someone asks you to explain what a capacitor is. Do you say:

    a. 'It introduces a delay into the circuit. Bigger capacitors cause a longer delay. It's a bit like a bucket filling up with water — big buckets take longer before they fill up and spill over'

    b. 'Is that the funny bit with the two wires sticking out?'

    c. 'Shove it into the mains, it won't electrocute you — or is it a resistor that does that? Try anyway. It's called 'testing a hypothesis'

67

Relationships With Parents

7. At a parents' evening a mother tells you that she does not feel her daughter is being stretched. Do you:

    a. Tell her you will make sure that more demanding work is set in future

    b   Express surprise that someone with a single figure IQ should have academic aspirations for her offspring

    c. Offer to buy her a rack

8. A father writes to you expressing his belief that his son's spelling errors are the result of dyslexia. Do you write back saying

    a. 'I shall refer him immediately to the educational psychologist so that we can get a statement and then buy in specialist help for him'

    b. 'A lot of children have been off school with it recently. Ask the doctor for some antibiotics'

    c. 'I cannot say I have been conshious of him makeing speling misstakes'

Relationships with Superiors

9. In your relationships with those above you, do you find that:

    a. You feel relaxed but respectful

    b. You get aggressive and insulting

    c. Your colleagues compare you with Kenneth Baker and nickname you 'Oilcan', 'King/Queen Smarmpot' or 'Grease Gun'

Extracurricular Activities

10. Once school is over do you:

    a. Run a chess club, several sports teams and produce a play or concert

    b. Break the British all-comers' 100 metre record down the school drive

    c. Moonlight as a bookie's runner and fleece the kids of their pocket money

Answer and scoring key

The correct answers are as follows:

1. You must always try to impress HMI, so the correct answer is (c), provided you point to your elbow, just to demonstrate you can tell it from other parts of your anatomy.

2. (a) is correct here, SEAC stands for the School Examinations and Assessment Council.

3. The odd one out is (a) SEAC. The others are all connected with education. NCC is the National Curriculum Council and BUM is what you sit on when you prepare your lessons.

4. You should have answered (b). By keeping the queue going until the bell you are doing an important piece of personal and social education, teaching children that queuing is an inescapable element of British life.

5. The correct answer here is (c), as you should have involved the head in helping you cover the attainment targets of the national curriculum in English which cover non-standard language and dialect forms. Some heads are an especially useful resource here.

6. You should have answered (a) to this question, unless your school is overcrowded, in which case (c) is the correct response, as every effort is made to reduce class sizes.

7. The only acceptable answer to this item is (b). Genetics is an important attainment target in the national curriculum for science.

8. A gesture must be made here. (c) is the answer which puts the spelling furore in perspective and confirms the stereotype that teachers do not care about spelling nor can they spell accurately themselves. Might as well keep a good media story going.

9. Oiling the system was Kenneth Baker's major contribution to education during his time at the DES, so answer (c) is correct as it preserves his memory.

10. Being able to run fast has become very important for teachers in the past few months after all the vitriolic attacks in the mass media, so (b) is correct.

Your appraisal

If you obtained fewer than five correct answers, then you are eligible for an Incentive Allowance Y, which stands for 'You Must Be Joking'. It consists of a '£5 off' voucher for the chairman of governors' out-of-town shopping mart.

A score of 6,7 or 8 entitles you to remission from reading the next 25 booklets from SEAC or the National Curriculum Council, a highly prized reward for all your efforts.

If you obtained 9 or 10 then you almost certainly have caught Mad Curriculum Disease, as only those suffering from it could have figured out the bizarre logic behind the test. Your prize is that you can have ten rounds of fisticuffs with Kenneth 'the Ninja' Clarke.

Times Educational Supplement 21.12.90

"IVE WORKED OUT YOUR MONTHLY SALARY UNDER THE NEW PERFORMANCE RELATED PAY SCHEME, FROBISHER, AND YOU OWE US £275..."

Beating classroom jitters

Every September, more than two million children either start school or transfer from one to another. For five-year-olds leaving home to spend much of their day in an infant school, or older children moving up to the senior school, some anxiety is inescapable.

Most of us can recall our own first day because images of it are etched deeply into the memory. I was the only child not to get a bottle of milk. There were 40 children and only 39 bottles of milk, so the new boy had to go without. Since then, whenever a courier announces there are 40 people on the bus, but only 39 theatre tickets, I know exactly whose name will be missing from the list.

In the weeks and months before young children start school, parents are tormented about what they should be doing to prepare them for it. There is a natural desire to make a modest start on education, perhaps do a little simple reading or writing, a few elementary sums, nothing too ambitious, just a switching-on of the ignition and a gentle warming up. On the other hand there is the fear of being too pushy or over-ambitious.

A few years ago I interviewed more than a hundred parents to ask what they did to prepare their children for school. Most said they had been told that parents who engaged in such pre-season training could damage their children. When we asked teachers what harm parents might do, we were given but one answer, parents teach capital letters and schools usually start with lower case.

Today, it is much more common for parents to be advised by teachers to think positively, to read to and with children, let them help with shopping so they learn about numbers and our money system, play family games and encourage children to talk and listen to others and to capitalise on their natural curiosity about the world around them. The only harm that could occur would be if parents made learning seem utterly odious.

Most primary schools encourage preliminary visiting by children in order to minimise the formality of the first day. Indeed it is common practice to phase two or three children into a new reception class at a time so the teacher can greet every newcomer.

Last September, as part of the Leverhulme Primary Project at Exeter University, we studied a number of primary classes for the first week of the school year. The class I observed consisted mainly of five-year-old beginners. Many seemed relaxed, some looked pale and tense, a few caused mayhem. Their parents were virtual replicas of the children.

The last arrival was a girl who screamed her way down the corridor accompanied by a distraught mother uttering oaths and bribes. The school had brought an extra teacher in for the day to help with difficult cases; the child promptly kicked her on the shin.

Minutes after her mother had departed, she was skilfully steered towards a table full of modelling equipment and she remained absorbed in various activities throughout the day.

When her mother arrived at 3.30, she promptly burst into tears, giving the impression, no doubt, that she had spent the day on the rack.

By the time that children transfer from primary to secondary school, they are familiar with schooling but not with their new school. In rural areas with small two or three-teacher primary schools, some pupils may move from being one of 50 to 100 pupils to being one of 1,000 or more.

The senior pupil from the primary school has suddenly become the most junior in the secondary school, unfamiliar with the rules, like a Martian landing on a rugby field. Wander off to the library to check some detail in a reference book, as you did in your primary school, and the teacher asks you why you are leaving the room or your seat without permission.

Many schools organise smooth transitions from primary to secondary. It is much more common today for secondary teachers, particularly those responsible for first years, to visit and even teach in feeder primary schools.

Open days for parents to visit are also more frequent, and many secondary schools arrange half or full day programmes for primary school pupils. This can offer them experiences they may not have had, such as a science lesson in a proper laboratory.

The biggest fear that many pupils express on transfer to a senior school is of bullying. Generations of pupils have gleefully passed on gruesome stories of savage initiation rites meted out to newcomers, the most persistent of which is that their heads will be flushed down the lavatory. So far as I know, no headless first-former has ever been seen in any British secondary school, and in any case where would the head actually go?

None the less, as with bogeymen and ghosts, this is not a rational matter, and both teachers and parents need to be sensitive to the fear.

The Times 20.8.90

Learning unlocked

What makes a good teacher is something that children, parents, administrators, policy makers, researchers and teachers themselves can speculate endlessly about. To some extent, the necessary characteristics will vary according to the individual and the circumstances. Someone attempting to instruct and inform an international conference of surgeons would not display exactly the same qualities as someone teaching a five-year-old to read, though there may be certain similarities.

Attempts to find universal 'good teacher' characteristics have usually failed because of these individual differences. There is no single stereotype since, and in the case of many of the qualities one can think of, there will always be someone who seems to achieve success without it. Being a world authority on subject matters might be a prerequisite for the international conference of surgeons, but it would be of little help to someone who could not keep 4C in order. A high degree of class control on the other hand, however valuable to someone taking 30 pupils, would not be essential for the musician teaching violin to a single, dedicated student.

The BBC2 series *The Transformers,* three one-hour documentaries on remarkable teachers who appear to have changed the lives of deprived children, has wisely avoided trying to pretend that they are all the same, and has instead presented in considerable detail the story of each of them. The three films are shot in different countries: the Soviet Union, Israel, and the United States, and each programme concentrates entirely on the individual case: the children's home near Moscow where deaf and blind children are taught; the Jerusalem location of Reuven Feuerstein's work; and Newark, New Jersey, where Matthew Lipman teaches philosophy to tough kids on the block.

The first of the three programmes, *The Butterflies of Zagorsk* tells of a children's home where the ideas of the Russian psychologist Lev Vygotsky are put into practice with children who are nearly, or entirely, blind and deaf. Vygotsky died in 1934, but his writings on language are still among the most inspirational sources of wisdom one can find. 'Language is power' the narrator tells us as we watch the rapid finger fluttering of children overcoming their intense sensory deprivation by using the language of hands, a complex-looking finger signing system.

One unifying feature of the three films is the refusal to give up or to accept that any child is beyond help. Vygotsky argued that language and thought are closely intertwined and lie at the very heart of learning. Even children of apparently very low ability could, he believed, learn effectively through skilful teaching. One of the early scenes in the film shows an assembly where each word spoken reaches every single child through rapid fluttering fingers in a large touch chain. It is a remarkable sight brilliantly filmed, as information ripples through the silent twilight of what are thought to be the unreachables. The feeling of emotional support for the children must be intense.

This intensity is shown specifically through the eyes of Natasha, one of the big successes of Zagorsk. Despite her multiple handicaps, she has trained as a psychologist and she writes poetry as well. Her dedicated husband, Yuri, escorts her gently through her difficulties. Another hero of the children has overcome his handicap to become a graduate and hold down a senior position. Former students constantly return to show the rest that there is hope.

One of two wider messages come out through the film. The first is that the Russians are not afraid to use a word like 'defective'. Indeed, the Moscow Institute of defectology has 18 laboratories, including one which specialises in this kind of work. Teachers of defectology are paid 25 per cent more than other teachers. It has become clear during the past few years, as more has become known of work in Moscow and in other Eastern European countries like Hungary, that there is a lot for us to learn from the best practice.

Another message is the importance of the multi-sensory approach with the handicapped. If people have lost most or all the use of certain of their senses, it is logical to sharpen up the others. Thus Natasha has learned to call on touch, smell and taste to judge the state of health or needs of her own baby.

One addition which would have helped this viewer would have been some film showing what the twilight world of these children feels like. Those of us blessed with reasonable sight and hearing find it hard to comprehend what near or total blindness and deafness really mean. It is possible to blank out the higher sound frequencies to create the low rumbling sound heard by those with a hearing loss, and also to soft focus and darken the visual image to show the fuzzy pictures seen by the partially sighted.

The only critical point which occurred to me is that the emotional music in the background sometimes introduced a note of unnecessary sentimentality. The girl seen at the end standing by the window wondering wistfully if she can every emulate Natasha, or whether she can ever find her Yuri, for the love of another is also an essential ingredient of success, is powerful enough, as is the sobering thought that changes in the Soviet Union put the whole enterprise at risk.

The second programme in the series, *Out of the Wilderness,* shows the work of Reuven Feuerstein, the 68 year-old white bearded Israeli psychologist, whose original inspiration came from the sight of Jewish children returning from refugee camps 40 years ago. I found this film less satisfactory than the others, perhaps because it seemed more pretentious in its claims. The early shot of Feuerstein being described as like an Old Testament prophet 'seized with a vision', accompanied by a picture of him looking down on the landscape from the top of a hill is faintly irritating. His commands to children to sit up straight reminded me a bit of my own early years in school, where this was regarded as a major virtue.

Certainly the scenes of disturbed children becoming more controlled and proficient are thought provoking, though the film never really makes clear what the children engaged in 'mediated learning experiences' are actually doing, beyond putting together or considering various shapes. The viewer could have done with a clear exposition of all this. Some of those shown look like bright children with behavioural problems which are unblocked perhaps as much by care and attention as by structured activity, though many are not in this category at all. One session on reading seemed to be little more than a straight phonics lesson on behavioural lines: small steps and immediate reinforcement.

Nevertheless, the work of Feuerstein has received considerable approval. One of my colleagues, educational psychologist Bob Burden, who has seen the work at first hand in Israel, is greatly impressed by the results. I prefer to reserve judgement.

The film I find most interesting, however, is the third one in the series, *Socrates For Six-Year-Olds,* which tells the story of Matthew Lipman, a philosopher who resigned his chair at Columbia University to teach philosophy to schoolchildren. Some of the most desperate moments in the programme are the street scenes in Newark, New Jersey, where crime and drug dealing are rife. Yet Matthew Lipman engages the minds of 14 and 15 year-olds from this unpromising background by inviting them to develop their powers of reasoning and expression.

Earlier in the film, a group of six-year-olds is seen participating in mature discussion about the nature of mind, and on such matters as whether they could exist without a brain. Lipman has written a series of children's stories which put philosophical propositions into concrete situations. The whole enterprise is an act of great courage and imagination and more than 5,000 American schools now teach philosophy along these lines. In the school featured centrally in the programme, none of the pupils intended to continue with education past the minimum school leaving age. By the end of the five-month programme all say they wish to go on. The true picture is, I suspect, slightly less spectacular, but the effects are impressive nevertheless.

All three of these films are worth watching, and they pose as many questions as they answer. One is: could we do it here? It would be a pity if experimentation were ruled out in favour of a dreary national curriculum sameness. A number of these ideas has been tried in British schools, Somerset, for example, reporting some satisfaction with Feuerstein's methods.

One is left wondering what best explains the success of the three approaches. Could it be the structure? or is it perhaps the immense enthusiasm, the care, the love in certain instances, the emphasis on the development of language, the joyous expectation of success, the exceptionally favourable staff-pupil ratio in the first two cases, or just the fact that adults are willing to listen and talk, that unlocks the world of learning for those thought not to inhabit it?

Times Educational Supplement 28.9.90

Coming of age

I remember the birth of Exeter College in 1970 very well, though at the time hardly anyone, myself included, thought there was anything especially significant about its being the country's first tertiary college. For all we knew, it could have been the last. During the past 21 years I have got to know the college both as a parent of two daughters who attended it, and professionally through observing and occasionally taking classes.

Back in the late 1960s, when comprehensive reorganisation fever swept the land, none of the schemes proclaimed in DES circular 10/65 had seemed to fit the needs of the historic city of Exeter with its 80,000 inhabitants. Unlike the 1980s when momentous Education Acts thundered out state required, legally enforced changes, the 1980s and 1970s were the decades of genteel DES circulars. 'This is only a suggestion, ladies and gentlemen, but do remember who is making it' was the general spirit of them.

It would be a nice fairy tale to pretend that Britain's first tertiary college was a visionary's lifetime dream, but the truth is less romantic. It was born of a mixture of logic, a touch of imagination — and expediency. In the late 1960s, Exeter had two grammar schools and five secondary moderns. The logical solution seemed to be the establishment of high schools for the under-16s, out of the secondary moderns and the old building which housed Bishop Blackall Girls' Grammar School, plus a showpiece sixth-form college in the newer building of the prestigious Hele's Boys' Grammar School.

This solution had the advantage of using existing buildings. It also got the powerful rugby-playing old boys of Hele's, mostly in prominent local positions, out of the city council's hair.

To be able to explain to some 16 stone Guinness breathing solicitor or estate agent, late on Saturday night, that his school had become a palace of learning, no doubt with a great rugby side, seemed less hazardous than trying to justify taking away its sixth form.

Unfortunately for the fire-eating old boys, the local HM Inspector was not impressed. What was the point of setting up a sixth-form college, when there were already A-level classes at the further education college? It would be a wasteful duplication. Taunton and St Austell later did precisely that.

The old boys were deeply dismayed. Send Hele's sixth formers to the tech? To the more traditionally minded, the tech was a down-market training place for rude mechanicals, set up after the First World War by a factory owner wanting better apprentices. It had, however, changed over the years, and acquired an imposing new multi-storey building.

Sucks to prejudice, was the HMI's view, so Britain's first tertiary college was born in 1970, in the multi-storey tech next to the fine statue of General Redvers Buller, the Boer War hero. As if by way of celebration, some students, discovering that the statue was hollow and full of West Country rain, drilled a small hole in his horse's nether regions. The steed piddled for a week.

Joyce Sherwani, a long-serving lecturer at the college, can recall vividly the dilemma facing the staff of the two grammar schools at the time. Back in 1970 she was head of physics at Bishop Blackall: 'We all had to apply for jobs. I didn't want things to change and a number of the married women stayed in the school to teach 12 to 16 year-olds, but my husband urged me to apply to the college. I've never regretted it.'

Joyce's career illustrates the changes in 16-plus education in Exeter in the past 21 years. The grammar school sixth-formers were phased in over four years, first the girls, then the boys. Joyce moved in on day one with the first cohort of lower-sixth girls and began as a physics lecturer, £5 per annum better off on the lecturers' salary scale. She is now the education officer at Exeter Prison — one of the college's many external commitments — and is used to jokes about lessons in safe-blowing. She organises courses ranging from basic English and maths to computing, languages, GCSE and Business and Technician Education Council. It is a big change from her role at the school and she loves it.

Alun Rees, head of physical education, is also a veteran from the grammar schools. He remembers the anxiety among staff of the boys' school: 'We hadn't a clue what 'tertiary college' actually meant. Most of the staff favoured a sixth-form college. We had joint meetings with the girls' school staff to fight the plan. There was a huge majority against it. Some of the die-hards thought it was the end of Utopia, but most staff were eventually happy with their placement. A lot of senior people came to the college, so that meant promotion for those who stayed in the schools.'

Like Joyce Sherwani, he has seen many changes: 'There was little PE at the old tech. I inherited a funny programme of what were called 'electives'. Students had to choose from 11 activities such as darts, snooker, badminton and guitar'. Today there are 58 activities, including most of the major and minor sports. Participants range from occasional enthusiasts to committed athletes like Darren Crompton, England Boys' rugby captain and member of the A-level physical education course. There are 153 full-time PE students taking awards ranging from GCSE to the BTEC diploma in leisure studies. All last year's A-level group passed and 89 per cent of the GCSE cohort obtained grades A to C. Alun Rees feels staff have become more professional with clear objectives and has no wish to turn back the clock.

A different veteran with no doubts is ex-Alderman Walter Daw, Conservative chairman of the education committee that took the plunge in 1970. Now well into his eighties, he has always looked down with earthy amusement at party squabbles. 'I brought everybody into it and we had meeting after meeting', he says in his rich Devon burr. 'I'd no time for bickering. I told 'em to take the politics out of it. Its turned out well, hasn't it?'

His reward was to be voted out of office by his colleagues, some of whom regarded him as wild revolutionary for supporting the scheme. He is still a strong supporter of the college, of which he has been a governor, and particularly admires the work of its two principals, Philip Merfield who set it up, and currently John Capey for broadening its scope. He is revered locally, while his former critics are forgotten.

Nothing could illustrate the diversity of Exeter College more than trying to find a 'typical' student in 1991. There simply isn't one. Well over 10,000 full and part-timers are taking courses in finance, law, social work, hotel and catering, agriculture, civil engineering, motor vehicle repair and maintenance, transportation, a wide-range of GCSEs or any of the 45 A-level courses on offer.

Natalie Wilkie, one of more than 1,200 full-time A-level students, 21 years ago might well have been at Bishop Blackall Girls' Grammar School taking her A-level physics with Joyce Sherwani. Instead she is studying maths, physics and art, regretting that she did not discover the college's great social life until her second year, and so missed a whole 12 months of parties and discos.

Now she is trying to obtain grades of AAB so that she can take up an offer to study architecture at Cambridge. The college is proud of its 80-plus per cent A-level pass rate. It seems odd that 21 years ago Exeter's director of education was so fearful the new tertiary college would be frowned on by higher education institutions as a horny-handed tech, that he wrote to every one explaining that the place would actually do A-levels.

By contrast, Melvyn Jordan at 52 is an interesting example of the part-time mature student willing to travel a long way to study. Trained originally in steel-making in Sheffield, he now works for Twinaplate in Truro, a firm specialising in timber and steel roof structures. Every Monday for the past four years, with the encouragement of his firm, he has made the 200 mile round trip up to Exeter to complete his Higher National Certificate and later

BTEC units in reinforced concrete and steelwork design so that he can become an associate member of the Institute of Structural Engineers.

'It works well both ways', he says. 'I can relate what I do in college to what happens in industry, and the college staff are very interested in the computer programs I've written and tried out at work. Programmers and engineers don't often get together, but you can here. I feel very well catered for and the staff are excellent'. A glutton for punishment, Melvyn plans to enrol in the BEng honours degree course in civil engineering which the college is starting up with Kingston Polytechnic. I suggested jokingly that he could probably knock off a PhD before he retired, but the serious look on his face told me I had just put another idea into his head. Why not? The nice thing about the human race is that you are only too old to learn when they finally screw the lid down on you.

Wandering around the several sites of the college is quite an experience. There are clapped-out huts, ancient former schools and more modern pur-pose-built accommodation on the main campus. The college has an excellent reputation in such fields as hotel and catering, a big employer of labour in the south-west. Eat in the training restaurant and no waterlogged over-salted soup will be slurped down your lapel by trembling trainees. There is a long waiting list for lunches and gourmet dinners, and standards are very high.

So they are in building crafts, where I met Sheila Brimacombe and Fay Blanch, the only two girls on the City and Guilds 588 craft certificate course in brickwork. There is still a shortage of girls in some traditionally male domains. Sheila and Fay had to develop external toughness. 'There are a lot of comments from the lads', says Sheila, 'but you give as good as you get. In the end they have to pack it in'.

When both girls walked off with the annual prizes for the best student there must have been some red faces among the acne brigade.

Such is the breadth of choice at the college that over 300 of its students have defected from the private sector, hardly surprising when you look at the A-levels on offer: all the usual ones plus law, philosophy, psychology, business studies, politics, Latin, accounts, sociology, and foreign languages — French, German, Italian, Russian and Spanish. For some, however, it is the mature atmosphere, the lack of uniform, regimentation or snobbery, that attracts.

Stephen Yeats left an independent school to study A-levels in maths and science at the college: 'There was a greater divide between the teachers and pupils than there is here. It was more starched. The final straw came when the bursar stood up in assembly and told us we were the cream of the nation's youth. I thought, 'I'm getting out of this, straight away'. They even sent the chaplain along to talk to me; well , perhaps he came of his own accord.' His first class at the college was quite a change, especially when his tutor began: 'My name's Pete, but you can call me what you like, as long as it's polite'.

This treatment of students as adults can be quite a shock for parents. I remember when college letters were sent to my own daughters, thinking: 'Hey, just a minute, how about writing to me? I'm only the bloody father after all.' Nor have I ever felt entirely relaxed at the freedom to wander into town when not in lectures. Why should my kids skive off into town? Damn it, at their age I was busy skiving in the school library, chatting to my mates instead of revising.

John Capey is adamant about the need to trust the students: 'At 16, yes, we'll communicate a bit more with parents, but at 17 and 18 they have to be given responsibility'. He has a formidable grasp of the whole range of tertiary education and a fierce pride in the college's achievements. He used to live round the corner from me and would occasionally pass me in his car when I was out for my morning run, pausing only to wave a friendly V sign at me through the window, so I respect his judgement.

But I still have reservations about the trust system. It works well enough for the children of professional parents prepared to put the boot in when the time comes, but my worry has always been for those with no tradition of further or higher education in the family. Won't they just slip away?

This is strenuously denied by the staff. Margaret Hawksley runs the staff development programme, and a lot of time is spent refining the 'key tutor' concept, first devised in the early 1970s. Each student designates one subject as the 'key' and a tutor in that field then takes special responsibility for pastoral care: 'Like others on the staff, I used to teach in a comprehensive and I think this is one of the strengths of tertiary colleges. You get people with that concern for the individual'.

Willie Neilsen did not come from a comprehensive school, however, and his responsibility for 750 students on what is effectively a Technical and Vocational Educational Initiative programme has alerted him to the problem: 'We've been monitoring this with the help of 20 undergraduates from the university school of education — and it's clear that many kids do find it a trauma when they leave the ordered, structured world of a school. I think we need a better induction programme. Some kids feel lost with this new sense of freedom'.

That illustrates to me one of the impressive features of Exeter College. It is good but not perfect. The staff recognise that and so ask their own questions. Are they truly tertiary, given that most students opt for either A-levels or vocational courses rather than a mix? Some staff argue that there should be more vocational elements in academic courses and a more academic content for the vocational courses. Should they introduce the British and International Baccalaureate or would that be a bit élitist? Have they become too managerial now that their size is so great? How will they cope with the free market introduced by the training credit scheme?

These seemed more important questions than the one I asked about the Government's recent announcement that it will take over control of FE funding from the local authorities from April 1993. The senior managers I spoke to were not unduly worried about the college's source of income and said there was already a degree of independence and a well-established governing body.

The story of Exeter College is an intriguing one, how a small city developed, partly by chance, a tertiary college system that was to become the model for 16-plus education in so many places — Nelson and Colne in 1972, under the resourceful David Moore, and cities such as Sheffield and Manchester faced with falling secondary numbers during the 1980s. Few Exeter citizens would now want a return to the old system.

Times Educational Supplement 26.4.91

None so blind as them that won't look

There is a scene in Bert Brecht's play *Life of Galileo* which has always stuck firmly in my mind. It comes at the moment when Galileo has been using, for the first time, a telescope to survey the heavens. He observes that the planet Jupiter usually has four visible moons, but that on occasion he can only see three. His conclusion is that the fourth moon has moved round the back of Jupiter, confirming that not all heavenly bodies revolve around the Earth but can circulate around the Sun and each other, thereby challenging existing beliefs in astronomy and theology.

The scene in question occurs when a group of people, including a mathematician, a theologian and a philosopher, comes to his house to check his theories. Galileo is convinced of the triumph of truth and reason. They will only have to peer through the telescope, he tells his colleagues, and they will be able to see with their own eyes what he has discovered. Unfortunately they spend the whole scene refusing his entreaties to look through the telescope, and finally leave to report him to the Inquisition.

This incident reminds me very much of those right-wing critics of education who show the greatest reluctance to go and look at the actual schools they criticise so readily. In recent years some of these have mounted a similarly ill-informed and vitriolic attack on teacher training. I have tried to persuade one or two of them to go and visit a few teacher training institutions, but with as much success as Galileo so far.

Consequently the criticisms from the right wing are written with an apparent but unjustified authority. The considerable press hype which accompanies the publication of pamphlets often gives their writings 'report' status, and some of the more gullible ministers and newspaper leader writers take on board their rantings as if they are based on true information. In reality they are riddled with myth.

One fantasy put out is that the need for training actually prevents good people from being recruited. Yet when maths and science graduates were allowed straight into schools without training in the 1970s and 1980s, more than 2,000 a year, many with higher degrees and good first degrees, chose to take a PGCE course and only a hundred or so entered untrained. Another is that training does nothing for people; that little knowledge is needed to teach in a primary school and that graduates with a decent knowledge of their subject can simply go into a classroom and start teaching. I have never been able to understand this contempt for training. I always fancy putting some hapless Nobel prizewinner in with 4D on a wet Friday afternoon to test this 'you only need to know your subject' view.

Some right-wingers seek to counter by arguing that a Nobel prizewinner in education would not be able to cope with 4D either. This is based on another false assumption that 'education' is abstruse theory. Education is intelligent action informed by analysis and reflection. Nobel prizewinners, therefore, ought to be well-informed and thoughtful practitioners, still experimenting and well able to teach a variety of classes.

A further myth is that teacher trainers are raving Marxists eager to implement discredited political theory on gullible trainees. Such matters as 'equal opportunities' and 'multicultural education' are seen as their own private creation. In reality such topics are Government policy and are actually required by the Government's own accrediting council.

Paradoxically one of the proposals from right-wing groups is to restore the pupil teacher notion of the 19th century, dispensing with training, and shoving young people straight into the very schools the same ideologues despise so much. It all seems so odd.

If only they would bring themselves to look through the telescope they would see that teacher training nowadays bears no resemblance to the fantasies they purvey. It does not involve trainees only learning one 'trendy' method of teaching and it is much more practically oriented than it was in the past.

A few people undoubtedly are gifted and widely experienced with people, perhaps in analogous jobs, and may learn to teach with relatively little external help, but anyone doubting the value of training only has to look at accounts of the effects of large numbers of untrained teachers in the 19th century to see what a disaster that was. Even as late as the 1960s, Mildred Collins did a comparison of trained and untrained teachers showing that untrained entrants were rated lower by heads; were absent more often; were more likely to fail their probation and often simply quit the profession.

There is another different training issue that I find even more bizarre. With some horror I learned recently of the system of training credits about to be foisted on the world of further education. It is market economics gone utterly mad. Each youngster entering training will be given a credit, a voucher effectively, ranging in value from £1,000 for National Vocational Qualification Level 1, up to over £4,000 for certain NVQ Level 3 courses.

The employer then uses this credit to train the newcomer, and though he can top up the voucher, as I understand it, if the training can be bought more cheaply he can keep the change. I can see some entrepreneurs making a very quick few bucks here. Furthermore, because the system is based on a set of competencies, virtually anyone can offer to provide these. I was astonished at some of the names on one list of approved providers I was shown: Flybynight Enterprises Inc, 122a High Street (over Greasy Joe's Chip Shop); Al Capone and Partners, Poste Restante, Cayman Islands; Spivs Plc, 12 Acacia Villas, (leave mail by second dustbin).

I can just imagine the state of the medical profession by now if someone had come up with this sort of training package a couple of hundred years ago. Among the list of competencies would have been 'Can stick leeches on bums', a competency faithfully 'delivered', for a few groats, by Ripoff and Partners and their successors right up to the present day.

Where is the investment, where the quality control, where the progress, and how can society trust a system driven by the profit motive and the market, rather than the need for quality?

Times Educational Supplement 5.4.91

Chapter 5

Teaching and the image makers

Phew! Standards plunge in silly season shocker

I was harmlessly walking down the street in mid-July, whistling a happy tune, when suddenly, out of the blue, standards starting falling. Crash! There goes a standard. Whoops! There goes another one. Look out! One on the left toppling over. Just like that, as Tommy Cooper might have said.

It was amazing how a period of relative tranquillity towards teachers and schools in the press, gave way this summer to one of the most vicious pieces of scapegoating seen for many years.

One minute teachers were at least OK, worth encouraging because of a possible shortage of recruits, the next minute they were responsible for bringing Britain to its knees.

As one hysterical account of slipping standards gave way to another, the dividing line between fantasy and reality grew ever more diffuse. Not for nothing is late July to early August known as the silly season. Had the Middle East crisis blown up three weeks earlier standards would have remained where they were back at the beginning of July.

It began with a story that a small group of educational psychologists had evidence that standards of reading among seven-year-olds in their area had fallen in the past five years. Unfortunately it was not possible to check whether this was correct or not because the data were unavailable. None the less many writers assumed (a) that it was true and (b) that it was all because of trendy teachers. Rhodes Boyson was dusted down and wheeled out to repeat exactly what he had said in 1972, when a subsequently discredited report claimed the same thing. Yes, sirree, Ole Baggy Eyes confirmed, it was indeed all down to trendy teachers.

Now hold on a second, little sunbeam. Go and stroll into some schools and ask yourself if 'trendy' is the word that most comes to mind when you clap eyes on a few teachers. 'Knackered' maybe, but trendy?

Perhaps I go to the wrong schools and all the shaven heads, purple hair and outrageous shoes are elsewhere, but the trendiest thing I ever see in a working week is the odd art nouveau elbow patch.

None the less this fiction soon became reified as teachers were divided into two groups, the trads and the trendies. Even the BBC flagship programme *Newsnight,* in what I thought was a disgraceful misrepresentation, fell into the trap. One newspaper rang me up to ask what percentage of teachers were 'phonics' and what percentage 'look and say', which was a bit like asking how many motorists drive in second gear and how many in third. I am still trying to find some of these stereotypes who sound out every single letter, no matter what the context, and say 'H-i-c-c-o-u-g-h equals hiccough'.

The next piece of 'evidence' of falling standards was from a teacher in Surrey claiming that standards of spelling had fallen in her sixth-form college in the past six years. Once more, although the full data were not available, the assumption was (a) that there was a nation-wide fall and (b) that it was all down to teachers not giving a fig about spelling, punctuation, written English or anything else. No one suggested that the college might have broadened its intake during the past six years, or that there might be an explanation other than duff teaching.

In the meantime, press coverage of an adult literacy report claimed that a quarter of young adults were illiterate. Really? One in four cannot read or write at all?

It was typical of the hysteria being generated as newspapers sought to outdo each other in the flagellation of the teaching profession. Even *The Guardian* has lurched severely to the Right in some of its education coverage, with the 'I taught in a London comprehensive and they threw condoms full of gravel at me ' and 'It's a great life in a Swiss finishing school' type of story. The occasional ranting leader and the Melanie Phillips columns further berate schools.

No one minds fair criticism, but the consequences of all this unjustified vitriol will be heavy. First of all the £2.2 million Saatchi and Saatchi campaigns to make teaching more attractive might as well have been flushed down the loo. The noise of disaffected teachers slamming the door on their profession will become deafening if the hate campaign continues in the mass media.

I feel particularly sorry for John MacGregor. I don't wish to ruin a good chap's career, but he is the first minister for years to listen intelligently and try to solve problems on the basis of what is actually happening, rather than dogma. Yet he is pilloried by press and colleagues.

Kenneth Baker, a Heathite when Heath was in power, a Thatcherite when Miss Piggy assumed the throne and, were Donald Duck to become Prime Minister, no doubt a fervent Duckite, has been privately putting the boot into him, giving unattributable press briefings accusing him of reneging on reform.

Consequently Mr MacGregor is pressed into putting right-wingers from the Centre for Policy Studies on to what are meant to be politically neutral national curriculum and examination councils, and given two new junior ministers who, however splendid, are immediately labelled as 'minders' by the press.

The final straw, therefore, was the announcement that Enid Blyton's Noddy stories were to be updated. Updated, for goodness' sake? What on earth can that mean? Will Toytown school opt out and become grant maintained? Will Noddy buy a Porsche and work for Mr and Mrs Tubby's merchant bank?

I was hoping to recover from Mad Curriculum Disease during the summer, but I am afraid that all this mixture of fact, fantasy, fairy tale, claim and counter-claim, has left my brain as addled as before. Did standards really fall one day in July and hit Chicken Licken on the head? Did Noddy and Big Ears become members of the National Curriculum Council and the SEAC? Or was it PC Plod who went on to the NCC along with Turkey Lurkey? Or did they become junior ministers? Is Kenneth Baker really Foxy Loxy?

R-r-r-r-r went Noddy's little red car as he set off to tackle level 5, attainment target 11 of the national science curriculum, only to find that Big Ears had become a licensed teacher at Toytown school. Big Ears knew nothing about magnetism, nor could he keep order. 'Dear me', said Noddy, stamping his foot angrily, 'Standards are falling again.'

Times Educational Supplement 7.9.90

Synchronised scapegoating by the Walden twins

A new explanation of the ills afflicting education is currently doing the rounds. It goes like this. The Government is putting plenty of money into schools, the reforms are absolutely terrific, not a flaw in sight, but they are being subverted by something called the Educational Establishment.

There is nothing unusual about all this. It is common, in human affairs, to seek some group or individual to whom one can attach blame. Children look for ghosts and bogymen to explain their undefined anxieties. Adults, especially those short on imagination, also try simple scapegoating.

This whole process is not a rational matter. When my daughter was small she was scared witless of tigers invading her bedroom. I tried to convince her that, round our way, tigers were about as commonplace as polar bears in the Sahara, but to no avail. It is not reason that is at work here.

Most of us have learned the art of stereotyping and scapegoating in our youth. As children we soon discover that wasps and bees can sting, so we develop a healthy respect for any black and yellow striped insect, whether noxious or not. Thus stereotyping can be an aid to survival, though its concentration on one or two salient characteristics may lead us astray.

This process of easy labelling was reinforced for me when I used to attend the local flea-pit on Saturday mornings to watch such B-movie heroes as Johnny Mack Brown, the clean-cut Savile Row archetypal good guy in the designer cowboy suit and impeccable white stetson. Hollywood simplified our search for the bad guys in life by making it obvious who they were.

In scene three, a crowd of unshaven thugs in shabby black stetsons, led by a Cro-Magnon Man called Jed Foley, or some such, would announce that the US Marshal was going to be run out of town. We would huddle together and munch our choc ices, safe in the knowledge that this powerful gang would eventually be seen off and that, in the last scene, Johnny Mack Brown would thump seven bells out of poor Jed Foley.

To return to the question of the Educational Establishment, some people must have seen even more of these dreadful B-movies than I did, because recently the quest for scapegoats has quickened noticeably. One or two journalists have rung me up to ask me if I belonged to the Educational Establishment, or, if not, whether I knew who did, or where they met.

The question seemed so utterly daft. As I understand it the Establishment usually consists of powerful people who control events and call the shots. I have always assumed they frequent the sort of London club that would throw scruffs like you and me out on to the pavement without demur. Power is the last thing that people working in education nowadays feel that they possess, as all advice has been ignored.

At this point in the story, step forward the Walden twins. Brian Walden certainly thinks he has discovered who the Educational Establishment is. Brian was formerly the star of that great Hollywood B-movie *Weekend World*. Like the Saturday morning cowboy films it always followed a rigid formula. In part one 'The Problem' would be defined via several interviews, each lasting precisely 45 seconds, with Brian reading his autocue in between.

Just before the adverts, Sensible Brian, who will be stereotyping for Britain in the 1991 World Scapegoating Championships in Helsinki, would announce that there were just three options open to Sir Keith, or whoever was the Jed Foley of the week. There were never two or four, always three. Sometimes, in order to meet the requirements of the formula, option three had to be: 'So the third option is that Sir Keith could do nothing'. The do-nothing option often had it. Then Sensible Brian, white stetson credentials now firmly established, would tell us to stay with him as he would be toasting Sir Keith after the break. Noises off as Sir Keith garrottes himself on his microphone wire.

A couple of weeks ago Sensible Brian, now starring in *Son of Weekend World,* or *Weekend World Rides Again,* I forget which, interviewed Jack Straw and told him that everything was the fault of teachers. 'And I know 'em', Brian announced confidently. Note the 'em', by the way, suggesting that good old Bri really does know his stuff, ever sitting in classrooms, attending in-service training days, giving a helping hand with the marking. It was the ultimate in crude scapegoating, and I fully expected him to say, 'Teachers, guv'nor? I'd string 'em all up. 'Ere, I once 'ad that Wonald Weagan in the back of my studio'. To his credit Jack Straw, like John MacGregor, refused to slag off the teaching profession.

A few days later it was time for *Walden 2,* as I found myself on *Newsnight* with George Walden, former education junior minister. George had absolutely no doubt at all about who the Educational Establishment was because I asked him. It was the whole of the teaching profession, academics like me, exam boards, and I cannot now remember whether he mentioned Harry Ramsbottom, the school caretaker and his dog Spot, who once cocked his leg up on a pile of national curriculum documents, but it seemed pretty all-inclusive — well over half a million people.

So it is time for us all to come clean now that George has found us out, and admit that we are, damn it, the much sought-after Educational Establishment. I personally think, George, that you should recognise that most teachers are busting a gut to make the national curriculum work, and that the source of some of the problems lies a bit nearer home, but you are quite right. We are indeed Lobby Ludd and you can claim your £5.

You might like to know that we all meet regularly of a Friday night. We tried the Albert Hall, but with 495,000 of us left out on the streets the police were not happy. Wembley Stadium wasn't much better, so we've taken to meeting on Salisbury Plain.

You're welcome to come along and joint the 'Ed Est', as we call ourselves, George. Remember that parking can be a bit tricky with so many of us, so I tend to leave the car at Bristol or Reading and walk in. Don't whatever you do, come in your white stetson, or you'll stand out a mile. Oh, and we have to be a bit careful about unwanted outsiders getting in, by the way, so this week's password is, keep it to yourself, 'Jed Foley'.

Times Educational Supplement 2.11.90

Potted version of Bill and Ben slapstick

There is occasionally a moment in life when the realisation that you are a fully paid-up Wally is inescapable. It is usually accompanied by an inner voice screaming in your ear, 'What the hell are you doing here, you idiot?'

It is something I have experienced myself on a number of occasions, the most recent of which was during a television programme which you may have seen a couple of weeks ago entitled *The Great Education Debate*. It was not great, there was not much education and it was certainly not a proper debate. In fact many of the teachers who appeared in it were, like me, not at all happy about it. Parts of it were so awful that there was a strong temptation to put a bag over one's head and talk like the flowerpot men.

There is a belief among some people in television that a jolly good way of having a balanced discussion is to set people against each other in a head-on adversarial way. The usual format is to line up a studio full of strident critics. After letting them have their say the camera crosses the studio to another group of people sitting behind a caption labelled 'The Complete and Utter Bastards Responsible for All This'.

What is interesting about these bear garden shows is the bits that the public does not see. I dislike watching or appearing in them, so I usually refuse invitations. I was rung up several times about *The Great Education Debate* and each time I said I did not want to be on it. I only agreed eventually because I was told that there would be so much criticism of teachers I was needed for 'balance', whatever that might mean.

Once the programme began my fears were confirmed. Only two out of 75 people sitting in the section labelled 'Parents' had anything positive to say about teachers. One of them, the chair of the National Confederation of Parent Teacher Associations, was howled down when she said that many of the six million members of PTAs were happy with their children's schooling.

The true atmosphere of a studio often does not come across on the small screen. When people speak they either have their own microphones or the sound is picked up by a highly directional mike. Viewers at home do not hear the actual studio sound because background noise tends to be shut out. At one stage Tessa Blackstone was being shouted down to such an extent I could not hear a word she was saying from just a few feet away. Yet television viewers only heard a muffled general sound of distant dissent.

The argument put forward by the programme-makers was that parents are very critical of schools, so it is fair enough to present education in this way. Yet in a recent survey of parents' options, Dr Martin Hughes of Exeter University found that, when asked if they were satisfied with their children's teachers, 83 per cent said anything from 'yes' to 'excellent', 16 per cent had mixed feelings and only 1 per cent said 'no'.

This was certainly not the mix in the 'Parents' part of the audience of *The Great Education Debate,* judging by the scorn coming from many of them whenever anything positive was said about teachers. I have been to numerous meetings of parents all over the country and have interviewed hundreds in their own home, including a number who were not happy with some aspect of their own children's education. The mood is rarely as portrayed in *The Great Education Debate,* and several of the ugliest scenes were edited out, as some 45 minutes of the original recording were dropped.

Three events after the programme confirmed my wish that I had worn a bag over my head and talked like the flowerpot men. One was the many teachers who left saying, 'We were stitched up, weren't we?' 'That will do wonders for teacher recruitment' and 'Why were we being set against each other, parents against teachers? We get on well together at my school'. A second was when I saw the camera script, written before the programme was recorded, which contained several references to 'Row between teachers and parents', confirming the confrontational intention of the programme.

The third event was when a couple of people from the 'Parents' section came over to me after the programme. 'We know who you are now. We've got your number. We know your face,' one of them proclaimed. Who was the 'we', I enquired, who had now got my number and knew who I was. He replied that the 'we ' was the Campaign for Real Education, the right-wing pressure group that had provided several members of the audience. Oh Flubba Lubba, as Bill and Ben used to say.

I don't know about you, but I get a bit annoyed when I see incredibly high cost of some day conferences. Charges like £60 or £80 per person are becoming commonplace, just for a single day, no accommodation. Over £100 is not unheard of, and a recently advertised course on SATs was asking £172.50, but, what a relief, that did include VAT.

I have asked a number of organisations how they justify such charges. The replies are very interesting. One told me that it included lunch, coffee, and a cup of tea and biscuits. Well that is convincing. They must serve caviare and give you the whole dinner service to take home. Another said it was 'overheads', so since the charge was over £100, presumably this one took place in the Sistine Chapel. No one claimed that they just wanted to make a large sum of money.

I do not know many people who can afford to go on these costly outings other than those in the first year of their inheritance, but I did manage to get some reaction from one person who had been on a £100 day. 'What was it like?' I enquired. 'Crap,' he replied, 'but it was delivered in very well modulated voices by men in nice three-piece suits, and we were all given a leatherette document case with someone's logo on it.'

I was especially enraged by the £172.50 for a one-day course on SATs. Since we cannot yet be sure what the SATs will eventually contain, it made me wonder what courses I could run about other hypotheticals. Perhaps £300 for my one-day course on 'GCSE questions in 1997' and £500 for 'What might happen at 10am on January 31 in the year 2035' could be popular. Caviare and chips and the chance to take part in a great education debate with Bill and Ben will be thrown in free.

Times Educational Supplement 30.11.90

READING SHOCKER
World Exclusive

In a *Sunday Globe* world exclusive we can reveal the truth about Britain's reading scandal. A specially commissioned *Globe* survey of teachers shows that a massive 88 per cent are very trendy and that a mere 12 per cent are what is termed 'slightly trendy'.

What is even worse, the *Globe* has obtained evidence that these trendy teachers are forcing Britain's children to read REAL BOOKS, a scandal which is rocking education to its very foundation. Today we name the twisted people behind the evil trend.

Our survey shows that reading REAL BOOKS:

- ☐ warps young minds
- ☐ makes you deaf
- ☐ leads to violent crime
- ☐ has killed millions

Every day in Britain's classrooms innocent children are reading a REAL BOOK and just keeling over, while trendy teachers laugh heartlessly at their distraught parents. Prime Minister John Major was uncompromising in his condemnation of trendy teachers when he heard the results of the *GLOBE* survey. 'It sounds somewhat disagreeable,' he said scathingly.

Names
We have learned that two evil foreign women are behind the REAL BOOKS scandal. Our enquiries reveal that British teachers used to be quite happy teaching by the 'phobics' method, that is the good old-fashioned sounding out of letters and saying, 'c-a-t equals dog'. Then they switched to 'look-and-speak' and started reading REAL BOOKS. As a result thousands of pupils caught Lassa fever or had heart attacks.

The two sinister svengalis behind the crazy foreign trend are Maria Montessori, an Italian, and Jean Rousseau, a French woman. Both must have gone to ground when they heard the *GLOBE* was on to them, as we could not track them down, but spaghetti freak Maria Montessori is known to have posed as a doctor.

Garlic-chewing Jean Rousseau is said to have forced Glenys Kinnock to read her book *Emile,* the story of a boy who liked look-and-tell and REAL BOOKS rather than phobics, and as a result thousands of British teachers became trendy overnight.

Campaign

Many experts have been horrified at our revelations. Albert Knuckle, president of the Smash Trendy Teachers Society, told us, 'Go on, what are you waiting for? Stamp out look-and-talk and REAL BOOKS once and for all.'

So today the *GLOBE* starts a campaign to stop Britain's children reading REAL BOOKS and get us back to phobics. We urge readers to do all they can to help. SO PLEASE, PLEASE.

- ☐ Stop children reading REAL BOOKS
- ☐ Turn them back into phobics
- ☐ keep buying the SUNDAY GLOBE

Ten ways to spot trendy teachers
They:
1. read REAL BOOKS

2. wear designer elbow patches

3. drive N-reg Hillman Imps

4. mark books in green Biro

5. wear old black shoes

6. call each other by their Christian names

7. belong to a union

8. don't read the *SUNDAY GLOBE*

9. can't spel proper

10. holiday in foreign countries.

Next Week: in the Glorious Globe. Punch a Trendy Teacher and WIN a prize. 2 Ford Fiestas and 15 Rottweilers to be given away FREE.

Times Educational Supplement 19.4.91

Not so much trendy as plain knackered

In the six months since I last went to the dentist for a check-up he has installed a fish tank. As I had to wait more than half an hour, it gave me a good chance to study this aquatic assortment. It was strikingly similar to the behaviour of those of us who work in education.

Some fish seemed to circle endlessly round the tank on what looked to be the same route. Perhaps they were doing the national fish curriculum. A bright blue one fizzed energetically back and forth, up and down, so far as I could see to no particular purpose. It reminded me of my own previous day. The biggest fish swam slowly around the top of the tank showering those below with its droppings. I looked in vain for a ministerial car.

I asked my dentist whether installing a fish tank to soothe the nerves of anxious patients, was the sort of thing that trendy dentists did nowadays. He looked baffled. The idea of being 'trendy' was alien to him. Whatever else dentists are accused of, trendiness is clearly not one of the charges.

Recently a teacher of plumbing at a college of further education explained to me how British plumbers would install a shower into the hot water circuit, unaware that the practice in other countries was to take it off the cold feed, avoiding numerous problems, like low pressure. He should start a society for trendy plumbers, I suggested. One never hears of trendy lawyers, trendy grocers, trendy engineers or trendy estate agents, only about trendy teachers.

What is it exactly about the teaching profession that has sparked off this hunt for the trendies? People like Lord Bullock and Lady Plowden have been named. This is sad, as I have found their weighty reports excellent for propping windows open on a windy day. It seems strange that a quest for fashion setters should start in the House of Lords. If you have not yet been called a trendy, then console yourself that you are still too young.

I had always understood the adjective 'trendy' to describe someone who follows slavishly and uncritically every latest wheeze, though given the vast number of these over the years, 'knackered' might be a better epithet for anyone so foolish. It is clear, however, that flitting from fad to fad is not the predominant meaning in the eyes of some users of the word.

It surely cannot mean someone who tries out a new idea or a different approach. I do not recall pioneers of transplant surgery being called trendy doctors. If teachers never tried out anything new they would be reduced to automata and children would never have learned about decimalisation and microcomputers before adults did, just two of the many unrecognised achievements by teachers willing to introduce novelty.

Recently it has been used as a synonym for 'child-centred', a diffuse concept frequently linked with statements about bad behaviour or low standards of achievement, as if these notions must inevitably cohere. The assumption is that teachers nowadays leave unruly children to teach themselves to read in the library. I have not met anyone who actually does that, and it sounds the obverse of child-centredness.

Putting the child more into the centre of the picture was an attempt to get away from the Victorian tradition of forcing children to chant mechanically things they did not understand. Books such as those written in the 1870s by people like the Reverend Brewer, involved children simply repeating phrases like, 'The climate of Britain is moist but healthy'. Try explaining that to the kids when it's peeing down on Blackpool beach.

If child-centred, however, simply means that teachers recognise the individual differences between pupils, that they encourage them to make decisions, to choose intelligently when there are options and to find certain things out for themselves, rather than wait for someone to tell them all the answers, then there is nothing recent about this at all.

That ancient Chinese Sage Confucius was far more of a trendy that I would ever want to be when he wrote in his *Analects,* 'I shall not teach until the pupils desire to know something... If out of the four corners of a subject I have dealt thoroughly with one corner and the pupils then cannot find out the other three for themselves, then I do not explain any more.'

Socrates, another raver if ever I saw one, 'that Greek git' to his critics, argued that no one can teach by transmitting knowledge mechanically from one person to another: 'The most that can be done is that one person who is more knowledgeable than another can, by asking a series of questions, stimulate the other to think, and so cause him to learn for himself.'

I do not myself actually agree with old Soccers. In the classrooms of the good teachers I see they use a range of teaching strategies, telling when necessary, asking questions, explaining patiently to those who are struggling, encouraging children to solve problems, listening, letting pupils work on when they are absorbed, and numerous others.

Last week I was teaching a group of seven-year-olds about magnetism. I could have given them a lecturette about magnets and their properties, asked them to write it down and learn it for homework. Instead I handed them a dozen different objects, like a piece of perspex, a nail, a copper rod, a pencil lead, a paper clip and a plastic rod. They were asked to sort these into two groups, a 'yes' and a 'no' pile, depending on whether they thought a magnet would pick them up or not. They were given a magnet to test out their theory and rearrange their two piles as necessary. Finally we compared findings and talked about what they had learned.

Was I being trendy? After all, I didn't just tell them things, they had to find out quite a lot. Or was I trad, because I had structured the activity? Did children misbehave because they were not seated in rows? No, they were completely absorbed. Were standards low? No, these seven-year-old now know far more about magnetism than their parents, many of whom wrongly believe that magnets pick up all metals. Was it child-centred, as it did recognise their different starting points and invite them to formulate their own conclusions? Does anyone really care about the label? I certainly don't.

Can we now decently bury the word 'trendy' which has become a catch-all term of abuse for teachers generally? Most important of all, do the fish in my dentist's fish tank have this kind of daft debate, or are they, as I suspect, far too sensible?

Times Educational Supplement 17.5.91

The teacher's Dilemma

If you see teachers looking glassy-eyed and lurching about unsteadily on their feet, they may be suffering from Pedagogical Spongiform Curriculitis, or Mad Curriculum Disease. They have probably been reading the countless folders, booklets and leaflets about the National Curriculum which have flooded through their letter boxes.

The core of the argument

The National Curriculum was introduced into schools in September 1989 with the three 'core subjects — maths, science and English. It is going to take the best part of the 1990s before all 10 subjects covered by the National Curriculum are taught as it dictates, as they are being phased into primary and secondary schools, starting with the first-year children in each, who are, respectively, now aged 5 and 11.

The maths and science syllabuses have been relatively uncontroversial. Quite a number of topics, or 'attainment targets' in National Curriculum jargon, were proposed by the working group and accepted by the Government. Fourteen topics are now supposed to be covered in maths, including such aspects as number, algebra, patterns and the handling of data and statistics. In science there are even more: 17 altogether, covering a very wide field from biology themes like 'the processes of life' to physical science topics such as electricity and magnetism, in addition to genetics, earth sciences and climatology.

The English syllabus favours a smaller range of themes, which includes reading, writing, listening and speaking. But when this first emerged in report form, it was controversial. Some journalists misrepresented the report as 'trendy' and against the use of standard English and the teaching of grammar. Yet the English proposals actually list the grammatical terms children need to know. What the report opposed was the ridiculing of children who spoke with a regional accent, and, as someone who speaks in the dulcet tones of downtown Sheffield, I was relieved to see this. In fact, the report and the resulting syllabus strongly endorse the need for children to learn standard English.

Strong foundations?

The seven other subjects are called 'foundation' subjects. I have my doubts about the design and technology syllabus, which was introduced this term. It is far too wide, covering not only technology, but also business studies, the use of micro computers and word processors, and home economics. My major worry is that cookery has been downgraded and there is too much emphasis on design and business applications. I would prefer it if children could enjoy cooking, rather than feeling they have to design a hamburger bar as well.

To many people's surprise, subjects like history and geography became controversial during the consultation period. It was partly because the Prime Minister made her views known about the choice of chairmen for the planning groups and the content of their reports, although political inter- ference in the curriculum has always been frowned upon. She wanted an explorer to chair the geography committee, but this proved difficult, since most explorers are striding across Antarctica rather than waiting to serve on a government committee. Then she asked for more British and less world history. In an attempt to please everybody, the history working group came up with a syllabus which was much too demanding at the junior-school stage.

Life at the chalkface

Even before reports are available from the working groups on subjects like music, art and physical education, primary teachers, in particular, are feeling under pressure. Many are not confident that they really know the subject matter they have to teach and they are unhappy about the amount of training they have received. The verdict from the teaching profession in general seems to be 'too much too fast'. In addition, many schools currently running on low budgets are worried that they will not be able to afford all the necessary books and equipment.

They are also worried about the national testing programme. The Govern- ment remains committed to national testing of all pupils at the ages of 7, 11, 14 and 16 by 1992. But the pilot tests have caused concern, especially at the 7-year-old stage. One headmistress said last April that she would sooner break the law than administer the proposed testing programme that she had been trying out. Still to be resolved are such matters as how to merge tests at the age of 16 years with the existing GCSE examination system.

It does seem a pity that the National Curriculum is becoming so bureau- cratic that teachers are finding it a strait-jacket rather than a helpful frame- work. There could, a few years from now, have been a genuine improvement in the teaching of science in the primary school, for example. But burying teachers under huge mounds of regulations is surely not the right way to achieve truly creative teaching.

Good Housekeeping October 1990

'Scapegoat' teachers face image problem

'SCHOOLS — the Great Success Story', 'I owe it all to my teachers', 'Education, the Backbone of the Nation'. Perhaps I lead a sheltered life, but these are just a few of the headlines I have *not* seen in the British press during the last few years. So far as many newspapers are concerned teachers have become the scapegoat for society's real or imagined ills, and have what Madison Avenue would call an 'image problem'. The gap between image and reality has become especially wide in recent months.

I see teaching in several contexts. First of all I am a teacher myself, and although most of my teaching is of undergraduate and postgraduate trainees, I also teach as often as I can in both primary and secondary schools. Secondly, my major research interest lies in the field of classroom interaction, and I have watched and analysed thousands of lessons during the last 25 years in a wide range of primary and secondary schools. Thirdly, I visit numerous schools to watch students on teaching practice, run in-service courses, present prizes, or discuss some matter of common concern with teachers.

Committed

Some of my best friends are teachers. 'Ah, but would you let your daughter marry one?' I hear you say. Well, yes I would actually, because many teachers are amongst the most committed to their fellows one is likely to meet. Although all of us know a few flinty-hearted members of the profession, the reality is that the great majority prepare their lessons, mark children's work, try to build up their self-steem and get very upset if anything tragic happens to one of their pupils.

Teachers are often portrayed in mass circulation newspapers as trendy permissives, running chaotic lessons in an anything-goes climate, not the slightest bit interested in spelling and punctuation, mindlessly following the latest fads, whatever they happen to be, and presiding over rapidly falling standards. It is unfair and inaccurate, but that is the image.

There is no doubt that teachers deeply resent the negative image accorded to what they know is an important profession. In a Teacher's Post survey a year ago, only seven per cent of teachers thought that media coverage of the profession was good or excellent. Most believed that none of the media represented their views properly to the public, though they felt radio gave fairer treatment than other mass media, which must have been good news for Wendy Jones, the BBC's excellent education reporter.

Stereotypes

Stereotyping is a common human activity. Because we can only process a limited amount of information, we sometimes group characteristics together, often allowing one or two of them to predominate. 'Thus if we learn in childhood that wasps and bees can sting us, we tend to avoid any buzzing insect with yellow and black stripes, whether it is harmful or not. Life can be full of stereotypes which may often be wholly inaccurate: malevolent mothers-in-law, garlic chewing Italians, doddering pensioners. Once the stereotype is established it is notoriously hard to shift.

It is strange how, even in childhood, children can learn to live with an image they know to be false. In popular comics teachers are still sometimes shown sporting gowns and mortarboards and carrying a large cane. Although a tiny number of traditionalists still may wear a gown, I suspect there is no-one left who wears a mortarboard to teach and who carries a cane, uttering phrases like, 'Come out, you little bounders' and eliciting replies like, 'Yarroo' and Cripes, chaps, Beaky's rumbled us'.

Some television series for children reinforce the notion of the teacher as a dotty anachronism or one of life's incompetents. 'Please Sir' was a series some years ago, occasionally repeated in feature length form, which showed teachers, in general, as sub-cretinous. 'Grange Hill' is one of the few programmes to portray teachers more realistically.

Politicians also reinforce the stereotype when it suits them. After the first of the urban riots William Whitelaw appeared on television and said, 'It makes you wonder what is happening in our schools', a response often repeated in discussions about football hooligans. Yet the truth of the matter is that most of the youths who rip up the terraces on Saturday afternoons, and appear to be beyond control of several hundred police, are quietly contained during the week by the very teachers said to be the cause of their bad behaviour.

Cartoons

Cartoons in popular newspapers tend to show teachers as shabbily dressed, wearing elbow patches, if male, and in tweeds and flat brogues if female. During the period of the teachers' industrial action, one television news programme showed for weeks the same graphic of a teacher standing in front of a black board as the archetypal 'teachers stand in front of the class and spout' image. The irony was the teacher shown in the picture had never taken part in industrial action, it was just an omni-purpose 'this is a typical teacher' picture from an agency.

Whenever I do television interviews, the director will ask for what is known as an 'establishing shot'. Almost invariably I am expected to sit at my desk reading a book. The only exception was a photographer from a popular tabloid who said. 'Do you prefer to be shown standing in front of your bookcase reading a large tome, or topless?' I think he was joking, but this all shows how stereotypes can be perpetuated through the mass media. Thus if teaching methods change and children work in groups or do projects, the 'Trendy permissiveness leads to falling standards' story appears to be true because teachers are supposed to stand at a blackboard, looking stern and presumably wielding a cane (even though a European Court of Human Rights judgement effectively outlawed corporal punishment five years ago).

Negative

There is no doubt that the constant repetition of negative publicity can have a serious effect on teachers' morale. Without a decent pay rise since 1974 overburdened with the demands of the national curriculum and local man-agement, opening the papers or switching on television and seeing yet another attack on the profession can be the final straw.

The succession of 'standards are falling' stories, most without proper substantiation, that appeared in the national press in the Summer, must have been accompanied by the deafening sound of classroom doors being slammed by teachers vowing never to return if they could find another job. Agencies specialising in finding alternative employment for teachers are said to be doing a roaring trade.

In order to counter this torrent of negative publicity, teachers and their leaders need to understand how and why the press operates as it does. Individual teachers can do little at national level, but a great deal at local level. The first message is that all schools must tell local newspapers and radio stations about the good that they do. One of our local papers once had a front page story headlined, 'Girl finds doll'. Well, that kind of thing can be big in our part of the world. Some local newspapers are so desperate for copy that good, if unspectacular stories about schools would be welcomed.

Newsworthy

This means that a well written press release is essential. It should be on one or at most two pages, tell the story clearly, and give a contact name and telephone number. It should also be sent to the newspaper or radio station in good time. No journalist can get a story into the paper at the last minute unless it is absolutely sensational. It should also offer a new angle, what a journalist would refer to as 'something sexy' (not literally, or it will be another gymslip story). If the pupils and teachers have helped elderly people, put on a play or done an enquiry into the need for a sports and leisure centre in the area, is there something newsworthy about it?

In addition it is worth liaising as closely as possible with parents and governors, especially when trouble can be anticipated. A good example here is the publication, from 1992 onwards, of national test scores for children at 7, 11, 14 and 16. The press could easily attack the whole teaching profession in general, and individual schools in particular with a 'Swinesville Primary School Bottom of League' story.

But if teachers have made the effort to inform parents and governors of what is involved in the testing, and how inappropriate the league table philosophy would be, then they have a much better chance of getting the public on their side. It will be too late in 1992 when the results actually come out. Now is the time to start, and it will be a wise investment of effort.

Teacher's Post, Autumn 1990

" SOME OF THE PARENTS ARE COMPLAINING
YOU'RE TOO TRENDY, MISS JENKINS... "

Chapter 6

Priceless primary schools

Polymath wanted: must like busking

The children may be smaller in primary schools than in other educational establishments, but that is the only little thing about primary education, for the figures are mind-blowing. In rounded terms we are talking about four million children with about 200,000 teachers in more than 20,000 schools. There are probably between six and seven million parents with children in primary schools and we have about a quarter of a million governors. Not so small fry when you put it that way.

Although there are on average about nine or ten teachers to every school, in practice the range is much greater. A county like Devon with its scattered rural communities, has 450 primary schools, of which some 200 have just two, three or four teachers. The challenges facing someone in the years ahead in a rural school with children aged between five and eight in the same class are not the same as those encountered by a teacher in an inner city school with pupils from several different communities, though there are similarities.

During the coming years the national curriculum will continue to dominate planning time. As more subjects are phased in through the school there will be more and more demands for teachers to update their own subject knowledge. As part of the Leverhulme Primary Project at Exeter University we have been studying teachers introducing topics such as technology or electricity for the first time. The real killer is children's questions. You can prepare a nice little scheme of work and then to be completely floored by the questions.

The first time I ever taught science to six and seven-year-olds I was asked, in the first minute, why cars were made of metal, why smoke came out of the back of a motor bike, why it snowed and why wagtails wagged their tails. It was nothing that a couple of lifetimes in the library could not have solved, but I was as competent to deal with it as perform a sub-frontal leucotomy.

We found that teachers prefer access to people rather than just books when on shaky ground, and in one case teachers got help from a local secondary school science teacher who came in once a month. It was a good model which highlights the vital roles of the subject co-ordinators in primary schools. Another teacher was helped by a governor and a different one by a parent with a scientific background. What a nice reversal that one was. Exasperated parents used to say to their children, 'Oh, leave me alone, go and ask your teacher'. Now it's the other way round.

The next subject problem is going to be key stage 2 history. Although the requirements have now been simplified, teachers will still need to have a considerable amount of historical knowledge, from ancient Greece to recent times. If you see people on the roof of Strangeways throwing tiles it will probably be jailed primary teachers wanting a copy of Trevelyan.

Another biggie will be national testing at seven and eleven. Try to stave off the league table approach to test scores by making sure that key people like parents, governors and journalists understand what is involved, and in good time.

It will be no use shedding tears once some idiot has given massive publicity to a crudely assembled league table in the local media.

Finally the issue of local management will continue to press, especially in schools that are short of cash. I hope that parents do not hold heads and teachers responsible for shortfalls in books and equipment, just because the school lacks cash. My advice here is twofold: first learn to busk, a most useful skill in our lucky dip society; second, keep smiling. The sense of humour in most primary staffrooms has headed off many nervous breakdowns.

Times Educational Supplement 11.1.91

Outcasts on the dark side of Pluto

'Yes, but what's actually *happening?*' The question came from a curious but frustrated 10-year-old in a class I was teaching about microelectronics. Working with kits in groups of four the children had to find the effect of putting different components into a circuit, in this case a capacitor.

When you put a capacitor into a circuit it introduces a delay, depending on its size. Press the switch and half a second, a second, or even more time elapses before the bulb lights up, according to the nature of the capacitor. That much I knew, but like many trying to teach primary science and technology, I was clueless about the nature of the process.

A helpful colleague later told me that the analogy of a bucket filling up with water might be helpful — little buckets fill up quickly and then overflow, big buckets take longer. I prayed silently the 10-year-old would not ask for more detail about what was inside the capacitor and wondered how good an analogy water would be. My grasp of the innards of a capacitor is about as profound as my knowledge of the dark side of Pluto.

As part of the Leverhulme Primary Project at Exeter University we are doing several case studies of teachers teaching topics like 'electricity' for the first time. We have also interviewed, and in some cases observed, more than 100 experienced teachers and trainees learning about teaching topics such as 'levers' and 'flotation' from the BBC videos on primary science.

At the start of the Leverhulme Project we conducted a nationwide survey of more than 900 primary teachers to find out how competent they felt with their existing subject knowledge.

Taking the nine subjects of the national curriculum, plus religious education, we were not too surprised to find that English was in first place, with more that 80 per cent confident they could tackle it without too much help. At the bottom end were science, music and technology. Only a third felt competent in science, a quarter in music, and a mere one in seven in technology.

I have observed teachers who are brilliant in most other fields struggling in science and technology, though often enjoying the experience of learning with the class. One teacher I saw began her first lesson by saying, 'Look, I have to be honest with you. I know nothing about electricity. I can just about change a fuse'.

When one group could not make the bulb light up she had to push them on to their own resources. A battery was the wrong way round, but correcting that still did not work. Suddenly there was a cry of, 'We've done it!' as someone found the bulb was not properly connected. It was a toss up which was greater, the excitement of the pupils or the relief of the teacher.

Talking to her afterwards brought out two important points, one plus and one minus. The positive side was that, had she been an expert in science, she might well have solved the problem for the children, instead of pressing them to find the answer themselves. The negative side is that one cannot trade on ignorance forever, for where would it stop? Brain surgery? 'I know nothing about brain surgery, but here's a scapel, there's a brain...'

The knowledge demands on primary teachers trying to cover the national curriculum are formidable. It is not just Boudicca and the rest in history over three different millennia, but scientific fields as diverse as forces, astronomy, genetics and earth sciences. Our research shows that teachers are keen to get to grips with the subjects, despite apprehension about their own lack of knowledge.

They are most keen to learn about physical science and scientific process topics, aspects of primary science often criticised by HM Inspectorate. 'We need the scientific principles pin-pointing', one teacher of seven to nine-year-olds told me.

She had been teaching flotation, but was unable to explain to the class why some grains of sand sink and others float, nor why a whole orange floats, but single slices of orange sink.

Videos can be an excellent source of help. The BBC primary science Inset videos have some brilliantly filmed scenes showing why lifeboats do not sink or how materials can be strengthened, and our research showed that teachers could actually learn quite valuable science from videos, as well as pick up clues or practical teaching ideas. But showing a video to a class can be a rigmarole, and one teacher explained how, with two helpers needed to cart all the gear to her part of the school, and then not always being able to find the right spot on the cassette, there were a few constraints.

Teachers value having people to answer their questions. One had explained how much help a local secondary teacher had been to her and her colleagues, as he came in once a month to answer queries. The role of the primary science co-ordinator is also crucial. One told us how he had produced his own booklet for staff based on BBC videos, highlighting the main teaching points, suggesting experiments and showing how it could all fit into cross-curricular topics being covered in class.

Most of all teachers need some time and training. Acquiring greater confidence and knowledge in science cannot be achieved overnight or on a one or two-day course.

We must have a big national effort to boost primary teachers' subject knowledge. They would certainly welcome it.

Times Educational Supplement 15.2.91

Thou shalt not covert they neighbour's answers

Rules, rules, rules. Wherever you look in primary classrooms there are rules. Even in schools which are fairly laid back about these things, children have to learn a set of conventions and rules that govern their daily lives.

As part of the Leverhulme Primary Project at Exeter University we have been looking at rules in our studies of class management. It is fascinating to see the similarities and differences in a variety of primary schools.

Many human activities are governed by rules. If we tried to drive a car, play chess or buy a house without following rules, there would be chaos.

Learning to understand, follow, sometimes make, and occasionally break rules is an important part of children's personal and social education.

One American study at the University of Houston identified 32 salient classroom rules, of which 22 had been spoken of by the teacher in the first six days of the year. Fifteen of these rules came from outside the classroom, usually from the head teacher.

We have found a similar situation in British primary schools. Local authorities usually decide the rules that govern safety on a school journey or during swimming lessons.

The school itself frequently has a policy on matters such as playground behaviour, running in the corridor or clothing, and then individual teachers decide how work will be set out or what kind of misbehaviour will not be tolerated in their classroom.

In addition the children may be invited to formulate or negotiate rules of different kinds. Conscious that to read out a list of 30 or 40 rules during the first minute of their first-ever lesson with a new class would probably empty the room, most teachers use a variety of strategies to establish ground rules.

I once came across a teacher who complained to the children that some of them 'had big eyes'. This apparently gratuitous insult to such revered figures as Walt Disney's Mickey Mouse turned out to be a coded message that she had spotted someone copying off a neighbour during a test.

Take for example the common classroom rule: 'Don't just call out, put your hand up if you want to say anything. 'One teacher may announce this on the first morning, another may wait until someone does call out and then explain how the rule works.

A third teacher may say: 'Let's think about what we're going to need to do so that we can all talk and listen to each other properly,' and then invite the children to make suggestions.

The rules we have observed most frequently concern movement (no running, ask if you want to leave the room), talking (only one person at a time, silence in the library, different levels of noise tolerated by different teachers), work (being independent, not distracting others), safety (care with scissors, no swinging on chairs), materials (where to put things, clothing and PE kit on pegs), social behaviour (be thoughtful about others, don't go into someone else's tray), and clothing (label clothes, what may or may not be worn).

It is quite remarkable how good teachers are able to establish such a complexity of rules and working conventions, often with quite young children sometimes with pupils from a very unruly background, without appearing to nag all the time, or be rigid and dictatorial, or resort to the ferocious punishments common during Victorian times.

I did encounter a sad event in America, however. At the beginning of the school year one teacher had a tree in the classroom, and every child's name was written on an autumn leaf. If you broke a rule your leaf was removed from the tree.

Just imagine, only seven-years-old and you're a dead leaf. What do you do for the rest of your life?

Times Educational Supplement 21.6.91

My old teacher

When I attended primary school in the late 1940s, the legacy of the war was still visible: large classes, dog-eared texts and exercise books full of what seemed to be blotting paper, making the lines of our writing spread inkily all over the page like a river estuary.

Shining like a beacon through these dreary mists was a teacher who, I realised later, was a pioneer of what became known as the Primary Revolution. George Long taught 51 of us for our last two years at Hunters' Bar Council School in Sheffield. Three quarters were working-class and a quarter came from the posher suburb up the hill, above the smog line. He was enthusiastic, well-organised, largely benign, but stern when necessary, and we all owe him an immeasurable debt.

Not only did George Long prepare this large and disparate class for the 11-plus, with an astonishing 70 per cent passing it, he also embarked on a series of ambitious projects and topics that signalled a new style for primary education. It became known as the 'drills and frills' approach: bung in the basics during the morning, do projects in the afternoon.

What we learn between the ages of nine and eleven often stays with us throughout our lives. I know York Minster inside out. We were all given a piece of it to study. My bit was the Five Sisters window, others had the nave, the transepts or the crypt. Each group addressed the class on our researches, and writings and drawings were mounted in a huge project book. When we visited York we knew more about the Minster than the guide did.

Years later I watched with horror the television pictures of the Minster in flames, wondering if the Five Sisters window was intact. I knew my contemporaries would be picturing George Long striding through the nave with 51 excited 10-year-olds.

We also chose individual projects. I researched the development of medicine, reading after school about Pasteur and Lister in the City Reference Library, to which he had wisely introduced us.

As with all the best teachers, his influence has been far-reaching. Those who went on to King Edward VII Grammar School used to astonish teachers by identifying architectural styles with ease. 'Who taught you that?' they would ask. 'Mr Long,' we replied. He must have been legendary.

Ten years after leaving, I trained as a teacher myself. A tutor commended my idea of letting children listen to *Fingal's Cave* and then paint the picture the music had evoked. It was a straight crib from another memorable George Long lesson. I later did a master's degree and doctorate, partly researched in the same city library to which he had introduced us, and would bump into contemporaries, still hooked on sniffing around books.

George Long went on to be a primary head and later a primary adviser. He taught me, indirectly, that children need a firm basis of knowledge, skills and understanding, but must also sate their immense curiosity, use their imagination, take on responsibility, work harmoniously with others. The current rather shabby debate about whether he should be labelled 'traditional' or 'progressive' seems utterly irrelevant.

Independent on Sunday, 24.2.91

It's a question of supply and demand

'Are you the supply? You'd better go and see Tina, the deputy head. Tina! The supply's arrived.'

'Oh, hello, are you the supply? Right, You're standing in for Mrs Jenkinson. If you look at the timetable on that wall over there you'll be able to jot down her classes. I know she has a third-year group first thing, because they're waiting in Room 27.'

Thousands of variations of this little ritual are enacted daily all over the country, as an unsung army of supply teachers fills the gaps left by teachers who are ill, attending courses or adjudicating national tests.

At Exeter University, we began studying supply teachers as part of the Leverhulme Primary Project because we were looking at class management, something supply teachers must become adept at, since they are always having to cope with a fresh group of children. It soon became apparent that their story was much broader.

Many schools would have ground to a halt during the last three or four head-spinning years had it not been for supply teachers. They underwrote the introduction of the GCSE, the National Curriculum and, where schools could afford it, the administration of tests of seven-year-olds.

A survey carried out in London in 1988 showed that, on a particular day, about 3 per cent of teachers were likely to be away for a long period, through ill health, pregnancy or leave of absence, and about 10 per cent for a shorter period, again through illness or perhaps because they were attending a training course. Only about 40 per cent of these vacancies are filled by supply teachers, however, as other teachers in the school are often expected to cover the rest.

The happiest supply teachers are often those on longer attachment who can get to know a school and become part of the community, but most of the teachers we interviewed had received the sudden early telephone call. One woman, well used to being sent for at short notice, lamented: 'It's the morning calls I really hate. My heart sinks. When the phone rings at about 7.40 you think: 'Nobody rings at 7.40 except headteachers.'

118

Another went to school one morning to deliver her own child and was collared by the head. 'Someone's not feeling well, can you do it?' Two minutes later she was teaching.

In the circumstances it is hardly surprising that teachers develop pretty deft footwork and some clever strategies. One primary specialist keeps two bags in her bedroom, a big children's bag and a little children's bag. As soon as the head has told her how old the pupils are, she grabs her precious holdall, crammed with paper, scissors, story books or whatever, and drives to the school. Have Curriculum — Will Travel.

The worst aspect is not knowing anyone's name, what the previous teacher has been doing or what the rules and conventions are. Children delight in playing up a new teacher: 'But Mr Jones always lets us play tennis in the classroom,' 'The board duster? Now let me see, no, sorry, can't remember where it's kept.'

One supply teacher was alarmed when a boy she had told off started throwing chairs around the room. 'Oh, didn't anyone tell you?' the deputy head said later. 'He's going to a special unit next week.'

So why do people do it? The major attractions are flexibility, variety and, for those looking for one, the opportunity to impress someone enough to land a permanent job. Financially, supply teaching offers a mixed blessing. The traditional method of remuneration was to pay about half a per cent of the annual salary per day, so that for someone earning £15,000 per annum, the daily rate of about £75, excluding weekends and school holidays, would add up to roughly the same after 40 weeks or so of work.

Supply teachers are bitter about moves to pay them hourly or employ some other device to make them less well off. Indeed, many of the people we interviewed felt the disadvantages of supply teaching far outweighed the advantages. They spoke of low status, low esteem and lack of training.

Ironically, one of their most frequent complaints was that they, the very people keeping schools going while teachers were attending courses on the National Curriculum, could not themselves go on such courses unless they gave up several days' salary. It was bizarre that they were expected to teach the National Curriculum, yet in many cases they could not even get hold of a syllabus.

'We are the lowest of the low,' was a common response, yet many were highly qualified and only worked on supply because of family or personal circumstances. Some children are being taught almost entirely by a succession of supply teachers in areas where schools cannot recruit enough teachers. It seems a rum way to treat such important people.

The Observer, 23.6.91

119

Does Dyslexia Exist

Dyslexia is a complex condition and may be inherited, as the Heseltine family knows. Like many who are affected, they know that despite cracks like 'Syd Lexia rules KO', dyslexia is no joke, and jibes about it being an excuse used by middle-class parents with stupid children are grossly unfair. It is possible to have language difficulties (the word dyslexia literally means 'difficulty with words') *and* a sharp intelligence, as Nelson Rockefeller, Albert Einstein, Michael Heseltine, and his son Rupert, all demonstrate.

So what can be done? Dyslexia is not a single disease with a single cause, but a set of symptoms indicating problems which need different kinds of help. Consider two 7-year-olds who have problems learning to read and write. Catherine has made little progress in reading and her speech is sometimes unclear. Alan tries hard to write, but gets letters and words back to front, and has a slight stammer. Are they both dyslexic? Well, yes — but the causes are quite different. Catherine is found to have 'glue ear', where mucus collects in the middle ear causing severe hearing loss, and delay in acquiring speech. Once her ears are drained, her hearing and speech improve and so, gradually, does her reading. Alan turns out to be a left-hander trying to write with his right hand. The confusion between left and right has made him uncoordinated, and the stammer indicates a language problem. He needs specialist help to decide if he should continue using his right hand and to show him how to hold his pen, and possibly speech therapy.

There are many other underlying causes of dyslexic symptoms, or Specific Learning Difficulties. They affect adults as well as children, and more males than females; there is often a family link. Some people have defective eyesight, others some kind of perception problem such as an inability to post shapes through correct slots. And of course, those with lower academic ability will take longer to learn to read and write — which does not mean that they may not be dyslexic as well! However, they all have some need in common, and the most successful teaching programmes will involve similar graded steps.

☐ Obtain a proper diagnosis to establish the cause of the difficulties.

☐ If difficulties persist after two years at school, insist upon specialist help. Educational psychologists will give an expert diagnosis and can be contacted via the local education authority or privately.

☐ Parents and schools must press for proper support. Individual help from a specialist teacher is invaluable.

☐ Everyone involved should work together and pull in the same direction.

Good Housekeeping, March 1991

Insulate yourself against the winter of our discontent

I love the autumn. It is the time when much of the best work is done in education, when solid foundations are laid. As I lurk around schools, looking for someone to give a spelling test to, there seems to be a distinct sense of purpose. Perhaps it is because, after the balmy evenings of summer, everyone can look forward to watching or listening to a few decent BBC comedies, like *Only Fools and Horses,* a series for people thinking about becoming licensed teachers, and *Today in Parliament.*

Autumn would not be quite the same without all the political party conferences. Perhaps Keats had just been to one when he described autumn as the season of mists and mellow fruitcakes. I love watching them because they are so predictable — the faint look of distaste on the faces of several senior politicians at the awfulness of some of their own supporters, the rising intonation of speakers who are about to utter the slogan which will get them a round of applause. No wonder some politicians think teaching is a push-over; they have just played to the easiest audience in the world, provided they voiced the right phrases.

Then there is my favourite, the debate with the most ringing calls: bring back the birch, lock them up for years, or at least put a curfew on them. Use electronic tagging so they can't go out at night. Life imprisonment should mean life. Let them dangle on the end of a rope.

I disagree. This is not the way to deal with teachers who don't give daily spelling tests.

As the parties tried to out-green each other, someone said the Government should give every school its own oak tree. Before you scoff, remember that this is a lot better than the usual tactic, which would be to give you an acorn and tell you to be patient. It is important to look on the positive side of things. With luck it will be uprooted in the next gale, demolishing the building, and the school can collect the insurance. Think what you could buy with £250.

One particular feature of this autumn has been the sterling attempts of authorities with recruitment problems to solve the teacher shortage crisis. Many overseas teachers are shocked by British teachers' low pay and long hours. No one has yet described it as a doddle.

It is interesting to read that the Dutch teachers recruited were given a one-week induction course before they arrived. I wonder what it covered. The location of the nearest soup kitchen? How to teach about circuit boards without any circuit boards? What to do when you are accused of everything from being the cause of football hooliganism to bringing Britain to its knees?

If it dealt with the national curriculum, then it was a week longer than many British teachers got. One Dutch teacher was sent home in the first month for hitting a pupil on the head, so perhaps it should have covered the right cross and the left hook.

Another issue, as the evenings draw in, is whether you should have installed double glazing while the summer offers were available. If one firm has its way customers may soon be dealing with teachers. As local authorities and governors struggle to find staff, a double glazing firm has been running its own recruitment campaign, mainly in the free sheets distributed to homes in the South of England, under the banner headline 'I used to be a teacher. Now I'm in a different class'.

The text runs: 'It didn't take a maths degree for Ted Urpens to add up that there was little money in teaching and that he would have to supplement his income with a part-time job. His landlady introduced him to someone who worked for Everest and he convinced Ted to give up teaching and go into Everest full-time.'

In the same naff prose style, making numerous plays on words connected with teaching, the ad explains how Ted 'took to the task in textbook fashion... the top of the class, you might say' and that, as a divisional manager, 'his salary, lifestyle and future expectations are like chalk and cheese compared to his teaching days!' The reader is then invited to phone him: 'He can teach you all about Everest, but it won't be on a blackboard.'

Surely the Department of Education and Science cannot stand by and watch the commercial world rubbing teachers' noses in it without fighting back. It is not time that a similar no-holds-barred campaign was waged in retaliation?

If the government is serious about recruiting teachers, let them first target estate agents. The headline should read: 'I used to be an estate agent. Now I'm in a *bijou* residence with leaking roof, er, sorry, olde worlde charm.' The text could run: 'It didn't take the sale of a clapped-out death-trap of a slum to a desperate newly-wed couple to convince Algernon Frodringham-Cholmondley that there was little satisfaction in being an estate agent. A member of his golf club introduced him to a teacher who moonlighted as a caddy, and he convinced Algernon to give up being an estate agent and become a teacher.

'Algernon took to the task in splendid neo-Georgian fashion and teaching became the freshly-painted alabaster portico of his life. In this much sought after profession he instructs his pupils, or 'vacant possessions' as he calls them affectionately, in the select, well-appointed shed next to the boiler house, er, I mean, sun loggia with *en suite* modern energy-efficient climatrium.

'Don't be gazumped. Mortgage your future now. Write to Algernon at the delightful leasehold property, Swinesville Opted-out Primary School, marking your envelope 'seriously deranged', or telephone him over any weekend at the Sir Keith Joseph Happy Valley Rest Home.'

That should do the trick.

Times Educational Supplement 19.10.90